FIRESIDE STORIES

Copyright © Helen and Wendy Brown 2021

ISBN Softcover: 978-06451104-0-1

All rights reserved. No part of this book may be reproduced or transmitted in any form or by any means, electronic, or mechanical, including photocopying, recording or by any information storage and retrieval system without the permission in writing by the copyright owner.

Unless otherwise stated Scriptures quoted here are from the King James Version (Authorised version). First published in 1611. Quoted from the KJV Classic Reference Bible, copyright 1983 by the Zondervan Corporation.

Any people depicted in stock imaginary provided by Shutterstock are models and are being used for illustration purposes only.

Published by: Reading Stones Publishing
Helen Brown & Wendy Wood
Cover Design: Wendy Wood
Photo Credits:
[1] Special thanks to Caboolture Historical Village for allowing us to take photos of their exhibits. (Photos by Wendy Brown)
[2] Photos supplied by Norman Morris and Family

For more copies contact the Publisher at:

Glenburnie Homestead
212 Glenburnie Road
ROB ROY NSW 2360
Mobile: 0422 577 663
Email: hbrown19561@gmail.com

FIRESIDE STORIES

Helen and Wendy Brown

Reading Stones Publishing

Our Family Tree

Samuel Morris (born Southampton, England, 13 January 1856) – became a Christian in 1888 before his marriage to Emily Piggot (21 March 1894).

He was a blacksmith by trade and worked in various locations until he arrived in Inverell, New South Wales, Australia.

Their children were: Eva, Alice, Eliza, Grace, Elsie, Wilfred, and Doris.

Wilfred (born Inverell 14 April 1904) married Elvie Gray (16 April 1930). Wilfred's parents paid his apprenticeship as a bootmaker and he carried on his own business in Otho Street, Inverell, until he went dairy farming at Dunreath on the Swanbrook Road just before World War II.

Their children were: Norman, Hilton, Rose, and Joy.

Norman (born Inverell 19 February 1931) married Jean Olwyn Deans (7 January 1956).

Their children were: Jean Helen (Brown), Alan, Lionel, Olwyn (Harris), and Ian.

Jean Helen (Born Mt Isa, 1956) married Kenneth Wayne Brown (7 January 1978).

Their children are Lynette, Wendy, Jennifer (Maybury), William, and Alexander

Sam's Story
As told by Sam Morris

I was born at Southampton, England (13th January 1856) but when two years old, my parents moved to London. There I was brought up, and as a boy had good desires to grow up a good man. I would not tell a lie for anything.

At about 11 or 12 I started work at an oil mill. (Oil would have been whale or another animal oil). I had to leave when the Factory Act came into force: which permitted no boy to be employed under thirteen years of age. (I understand he was out of work for a fortnight until he turned 13).

[1] Steam engine showing rivets.

I went to work, however, at a boiler maker's shop as a rivet boy. A rivet boy worked inside the boiler, he would put a red-hot rivet through the hole in the boiler – then the boy had to press the rivet with a "dolly" (the boy put his arm through the ring until it was above the elbow and his hand held the bar below the head) while the blacksmith belted the rivet with a sledgehammer until it spread to make it watertight. (My dad said, 'it was little wonder that he went deaf in his latter years").

This is the "dolly" Sam used

Up to this time I did not know the taste of strong drink. I was about 15 years old when my parents left me in the east end of London and removed to Wimbledon – a few miles out of town. Thrown upon myself, I began to keep bad company and took the drink; and in a very short time became a drunkard. By the time I was 17, I could go the pace as fast as any of my pals, who were some of the fastest to be found in the east end of London.

At 18 years I learned blacksmithing. There I got mixed up with men who were unbelievers, who said there was nothing beyond this life. Their influence bore upon me and I began to think as they did; because I saw others who said they were Christians while their lives proved the contrary.

The men I worked with told me I would die in a ditch if I did not pull up. It was an unwritten law, that as a blacksmith, if you were hard up you could go to any Blacksmith shop, and they would give you a pot of beer, a hunk of cheese, or a sandwich.

[1] Blacksmith shop

One day, after I had been drinking heavily, I went back after work to the place where I was working, took a horse, and led him through the workshops, he was a terror for kicking, which he did, doing considerable damage to the equipment such as leather and wood billows, bags of coal, and tool racks, to the distress of all the men who worked there, and then I put him back in the stable.

The next morning, rather than face the sack, I started by boat to Hull in Yorkshire to avoid the repercussion and began to do my first bit of pick and shovel work. Thus began a roaming life, wandering to and from London and working in a great many blacksmiths' shops and never stopping long in one place. At one, I was driving a Boiler Pumping Engine at night, and took some beer down with me – which I drank and soon fell asleep. When I woke, the water was so low I was afraid if I put the feed pump on, I would blow her up; I charged it anyway and it turned out alright.

I kept wandering about, working around London in spite of my father's offer to set me up in business as a blacksmith. He did not know of my unfit condition. I refused, preferring to work at the different shops and drinking all I earned.

My father and brother made up their minds to go to Australia; my mother was to follow later. I would like to say here that, although I was so wild and reckless, I always had a great love for my mother, who was the only person that exercised any restraint on me. (Sam carried a canary from the North of England to the South as a gift for his mother, stopping at Blacksmiths shops, using the unwritten law on the way). I thought a change would be good for me, so I took this chance to go round and say goodbye to my pals, telling them I was going to Australia for a change of air. They replied there would be no fear of my going as I would not be able to get enough money to go.

But I went! Father loaned me the passage money and we sailed in January. Just before we left the dock, I spent the last shilling on beer, not expecting to get any money till we landed. It would be around four months before we would arrive in Melbourne.

[1] Model of sailing ship "The Mermaid"

Going through the English Channel it blew a gale of wind and carried away one of the yard arms; and the Captain asked if there was a blacksmith among the passengers. I started work and got beer all the way out; and had some money in my pocket when I landed in Melbourne.

There I had my first drink in Australia, and then went to Sydney and from there up country. I usually had a spell of work and then a spell of drinking. One day, on coming to town, a week or two before Christmas, I wanted to keep sober and went to work for a blacksmith. Before night I was drunk.

Then came another long journey from Wellington to Tenterfield; the railway line was then being built from Tenterfield to the borders of Queensland. I worked at Tenterfield for a time, then went on; travelled to Richmond River, NSW and back to Sydney. (*Sam had tricks, like wriggling his ears and pulling faces which sent passengers into fits of laughter. While travelling on the train they passed by trees that had been rung-barked. When the bark came off, they were left white. He said to a lady who was obviously an old time Australian, in his cockney English voice, Lady, who white-washed all the trees? She made a long explanation. He had rung-barked many trees himself*). From there I went up country but when I got to Glen Innes, I had no ticket; so, they detained me until I got the money for the fare. When the lock-up keeper asked what religion I was, I told him, "None – nor did I want any".

On one occasion while at Inverell, before a bridge was over the McIntyre River, I wanted to get to a shop on the other side of the river. The bank was very steep, and they told me I would never get up the bank. I put the horse to it. Well, the horse got up alright – but I stood on my head when I came off his behind.

Another time, when on a drinking bender with a pal of mine, being short of beds, we had a bunk between us, He took the top part and I slept underneath on the floor.

When the Salvation Army came to Inverell, I went to have a look. Someone asked me my opinion about the Officers, and I said the Captain ought to work and the Lieutenant wanted feeding up a bit.

On one occasion, when meeting the members of the Salvation Army marching to their hall after having an outdoor service, I tried to put my horse over them, but he would not go; and I have always said he had more sense than I had. On another occasion, my friends saw me galloping out of town. As long as they could hear me, I was galloping. They thought I would kill myself. Shortly after this, while riding a horse very fast and being tipsy, I ran into a buggy crossing the street. I was rather badly hurt. I thought I was done for, hard work would probably not be possible anymore, and so I thought I might go for a shepherd's job or something of the kind. I was feeling so down, I wanted to have a few more drinks and then die – the sooner the better. Explanation: Shepherds were employed to keep the sheep at the time before the fences were up. (One of Inverell Station's shepherds was still alive when we lived at Dunreath.)

After getting about again, I went into the Army hall, drunk as usual, and one of the members came and spoke to me, telling me about the saving grace of God. I told him I did not believe in God and wanted nothing to do with Him. But he said that God had saved him, I knew he was one of the biggest drunks in the town. I was impressed and by some means I went to the front for prayer. Several choruses were sung, and somebody prayed; but being in a muddled state, I did not get right with God then. I got up and left town the same night. The next day, while at work, there came to my mind the chorus the Salvationists had sung while I was being prayed for:

I do believe, I will believe
That Jesus died for me
That on the cross he shed His blood
From sin to set me free.

I said to myself *I don't believe it*, but I could not get rid of the words all the same. Then I began to think that, if Jesus died for me, He died for an unthankful man and the prayer came into my heart, *Lord, I do believe, help thou my unbelief.*

I started in earnest to seek God's salvation. I acknowledged to those about me that I was determined to live a good life, and if there was salvation for me, I would get it. I gave up drink. Several weeks passed by but I got no insight. One night, as I sat by the campfire (alcoholics are often loners, camping or living on their own) – thinking of Christ and His death on the cross, I had a vision of Jesus on the cross in the campfire, and as I looked, it seemed as if He was looking at me. It brought tears to my eyes, and I promised I would love and serve Him. Still, the peace did not come, and I was made to feel my sins more and more.

One night, the night Captain, Bob Smith, took charge of the Corps and he asked me if I was saved. I said I was not; but I wished I was. He told me to keep on praying and believing.

That Sunday night, December 22nd, 1888, I had a dream and awoke. I was still thinking of the dream when I heard a voice say distinctly, "Get up and ask God for what you want." I obeyed and prayed. Then the burden of my sins was removed, and the glory of God's salvation streamed into my soul. The spirit of God bore witness with mine that I was born of God, and I finally had peace.

The devil suggested to me that I should not tell anyone, as I would soon be back drinking again, but I promised him, that no matter how he might try to trip me up, I would rise again to serve the Lord. I was so happy after the change had been made in my heart that at daylight I was up, with the intention to go and see Captain Smith and tell him God had saved me – but being so early I went for a ride around the town. I could tell no one was up because in those days smoke had to come out of the chimney even to boil the kettle and this was the way you could tell if someone was awake. I went to the hotel and had breakfast. Everything seemed to be altered; I was happy. After breakfast, I went to see the Captain, and he rejoiced with me over the great salvation God had given me. He asked me to pray, but I told him I couldn't. Nevertheless, I made the attempt and he told me afterwards that when I got started, he thought I would never stop!

I stayed in town for Christmas, being the first sober Christmas I had in Australia. A few days afterwards, I went to see an old chum to tell him what God had done for me and that He could do the same for him. I did not succeed in convincing him.

Shortly after I was saved, I met an old friend; he asked me to come and have a drink. I told him I had given it up. "Yes," he said, "till you get your cheque". When I told him I had my cheque, he looked very surprised and shook his head.

I gladly testified to God's saving grace and keeping power, to the astonishment of many. One man, at least, said it would not last long. On Sunday at Kneedrill (7am prayer meeting) the Captain gave me the Articles of War (conditions for membership of the Salvation Army) to sign, I returned them at the next meeting and told the Captain that there was nothing there but what a Christian should do; but that I did not want to be sworn in that day. After dinner, I went to my room to pray and then God made it clear to me that He wanted me to be a Salvation Army Soldier.

On my way to the evening service, I met the Salvation Army, which had held an Open-Air service before they marched to their hall, coming round the corner of the street, so I fell into line beside soldier, Bricky Brice, the man who was saved while working at his grindstone in a workshop, and I committed myself to being part of the Army that evening.

My mother said that I would never wear the Guernsey, (The Salvation Army red jumper) as I did not like bright colours; but behold all was altered; I soon got a Guernsey – red! A few Sundays later, I met an old chum.
"Ah," he says, "you have changed your colours."
"Yes, how about you come to a meeting."
"No, they might catch me."
"Well, it certainly would not be a bad catch for you to be saved from Hell." I concluded.
So, I often had talks with him about his soul, and one day he came to a meeting and stayed for the Prayer Meeting held afterwards. Someone went and spoke to him, and he told him to mind his own business. He was sitting very near the front and was the worse for drink. Suddenly, I heard a great thump! Opening my eyes, I saw my old friend kneeling at the penitent form (a bench at the front of the hall where they could pray). I shouted Glory to God! He got saved and is standing true at the time of writing.

There were some big sinners saved during the Captain's term. One, John Coates, dreamed of the Army one night while he slept in the wine shop, came to the meeting, and got saved. The Captain's wife helped him on with a guernsey, but that night he could not get it off, - so had to sleep in it! When he woke in the morning, he felt so good he had to look in the mirror to see if forgiveness made any difference to his face. He grew as a Christian, developed his musical skills, and become a Bandsman.

Another man that I had on one occasion drunk with, had delirium tremors and spent some time in hospital. I met him after I was saved and told him of the love of God. He said he was all right as he had signed the pledge. He was surprised to see me as a Bandsman, and said he thought I was too funny a fellow to ever get saved! I lost sight of him for some time. One night, as I was keeping the door. (Keeping the door in those days was to keep the troublemakers out. There was some kind of grill across the entrance, and the ruffians used to put pins in sticks and poke them into grandfather through the grill. Also, they were such a problem, that when the worshippers arrived at the hall, they had to take their saddles off their horses, carry them over their heads and store them in the back room for safety). A man walked down the aisle, whom I thought I should know, and I found it was the same man. I had a talk with him, and he told me the drink was getting the best of him again. I pointed out to him that his only hope was Jesus. He came out to the penitent form and got gloriously saved. I have often heard him telling how God saved him with tears running down his face with gladness.

Sometime after my conversion, I had a feeling that God wanted me to be a Salvation Army Officer but felt, as my previous life had left my body damaged, I would be no good. There were three of us working together, who had been converted within a few months. One had offered himself as an officer and been accepted. One day, as I was thinking of Jack and the opportunity he would have of working for God, a desire to do the same came to me. I lifted my heart to God and said 'O lord, send me. The answer came to me, while reading in my Bible of the demon possessed man. Mark 5:19 spoke to me clearly. "Go tell your friends and neighbours what great things God has done for you". I then had the conviction I was to stay in Inverell. (He took his calling so seriously, that he never took a holiday away from Inverell.)

Being satisfied that my place was there, I settled down as a soldier and was made a local Officer (elder) after the first twelve months of soldiership. The late Adjutant, Plevin, (a staff officer, the equivalent to a Pastor in charge of the Church) was a great help to me spiritually while stationed here. He was holding on here alone for a good many months, and he used to call me his lieutenant. Many a good time we had at meetings and in other ways, and when he went away, he left me stronger in the Lord than when he came.

We had several outposts where we held meetings, and I used to go there to assist. At one place it was rumoured we were to be thrown in the creek if we came there. However, when Sunday came, two of us went. As we came up to Swanbrook Creek, several horsemen met us and rode past and back again, but no attempt was made to put us in the creek. They came to the meeting and behaved themselves. (Swanbrook Creek had a school. That was where the older Gray girls used to walk through the bush about four miles from Nullamanna road. Grandfather Gray had marked the trees with an axe, so they would not get lost. There must have been quite a settlement at Swanbrook Creek. When living at Dunreath, we boys used to ride our horses down there, looking at the old relics that were left on what was then the stock reserves. These villages, Long Plain and Swanbrook, have just become 'districts' with the advent of modern transport.)

[2] Sam and Emily Morris

I have often, when working out of town, ridden over twenty miles, and sometimes thirty, to a meeting and back again, and started work with the rest of the men in the morning. For some time, I did it every Saturday morning and back again by Monday morning. (Grandfather had an outstanding grey horse, called Neddy. He had caught him out of a mob of brumbies on Fern Hill. Sam worked down towards Warialda. This horse was such a good traveller enabling Sam to do it. He would do that distance up and back on each weekend. The horse had a 'show-off' streak in him – when he came to a number of houses, such as Long Plain, where there was a hall, school, general store, and post office, plus a number of houses in those days, Neddy would put his head up, ears forward, look about and dance around. Once they were past where the buildings ended, he put his head down and ambled at a fast gait. Some years later, Sam sold his wonderful horse, Neddy, which he had a love for, because he felt it could take away some of his love for Jesus Christ.)

Being satisfied that I was to stay in Inverell, I thought a companion for life would help me, so I took a wife, a good Godly salvationist and never regretted that choice. My wife was Emily Pigott. Her father was a Methodist lay preacher who owned an orchard of specialty oranges seven miles out of Inverell on the Bundarra Road. He was also a Councillor in the Bundarra Shire, and head of a highly respected family. Alice (later Mrs. Chisholm of Auburn Vale Road) and Emily, together with friends walked the seven miles to attend the Salvation Army meetings at Inverell. The girls have been known to sleep on boxes, so as to be early enough to walk in for the seven am prayer meeting.

When Emily consented to be my wife, her father was not pleased his girl was to marry a man with such a bad past, even though he'd been converted and was a devout Christian for some years. He refused to give her away and did not attend the wedding. Once we were married, he accepted me into the family. Years later, we lived on the property in what was called the Honey House, while we built our home in William Street.

Postscript: Where they lived and worked in their first years of married life has been lost! But we do know of one job Sam had, which was standing knee to waist deep in Gillespie's crossing, shovelling clean, washed gravel into drays. The gravel lodged there after each fresh in the river. The crossing was on the left of the little foot bridge, below the town band hall, over to the black flat. We still crossed there with horse and cart when I was a boy.

It is known that their first two children, Eva Florence, and Alice were lost to Diphtheria, and they nearly lost a third with that disease. They had their sorrows and trials, but faith in Jesus Christ would have been their strength.

The next record we have of the family, is living in a slab house on a farm that is now known as the Private Aerodrome on the Glen Innes Road. It was on this farm where my father was born on 14th April 1904.

Sam's diary in 1902 reads:
Sales:
        5 Pigs   £5.0.0
        3 ½ dozen eggs   5.3
        2 fowls   2.9

4 pigs	£1.0.0	

Expenses:
Paint & Repairs to Buggy	£3.7.6	
New Set of Harness	£6.0.0	

In 1907 it reads:
Sales:
6 pigs	£1.13.0	
1 pig	£1.15.0	
3 bags Chaff	15.0	

Expenses:
Wheat Harvesting	£1.6.0	
Youth Wages and keep	14.0	
6 plough shears	6.0	
Saddle done up	£1.9.9	

One of Sam's answers to prayer, while there on the farm, was when they had a good crop of wheat. I understand that it was 40 acres, a big crop in those days. – No hail insurance was available. A hailstorm was coming from the east. He went into his bedroom and prayed. "Lord, I don't want the money from the wheat crop for myself but to pay the bills at the General Store, because the owner has carried me, giving me credit on the strength of the crop." The hailstorm came to the Eastern boundary, went along the Northern boundary, back up the Western boundary, leaving the crop untouched, proving that God did it. Then he gave a prayer of thanks and praise and had a miracle to talk about.

[2] Sam's Plough

They'd spent some happy years together when a sickness that lasted more than a year came while they were still on the farm. The fact that he was a good gardener got them through financially, by the sale of produce. His feet and legs were swollen – he felt led to sit with his feet in buckets of salt water. He said, "I think all the bad things I've drunk and eaten came out of my body in that time. It was a time when my salvation proved good, everything looked dark, yet I felt I could trust God, and His presence was very real to me. Some of the comrades rallied round me and helped me in a practical manner, and also with their prayers. At one time I thought I was very near the valley of death, but I had no fear and felt I could trust my wife and little ones to God. From that time on, I began to get better, and although for years I was weak, today I am enjoying good health and I thank God for it. Through all this, my wife and I had many happy years together."

[2] The House in William Street

It was after that they built a house in William Street, on a large block of land with room for a cow, horse, poultry and a large garden.

After they moved into William Street, their only son, Wilfred, had appendicitis (before operations were practiced). It was known as 'Inflammation of the bowel'. Wilfred was my dad and told me he did not know how long he was unconscious, but when he 'came to' he could feel his ribs as if they were about to stick through his skin. He was 12 months late starting school. That would have tried Sam and Emily's faith. Sam's last job for years, was Head Gardener of the Victoria Park in Vivian Street. He had a gracious way of dealing with vandals. He had a large sunken garden in the centre of the park as a feature. Every night a troublemaker would walk straight through the centre, damaging the plants. Sam soaked the garden all day, so the black soil was turned to 'slop'. The next day, there were several steps into the slop and then out again. No more trouble.

My mother believed that the families who came into the Salvation Army at Inverell from Bible believing Churches, some of which were Barnes, Truman's, Pigott's, and Gray's, gave the Corps stability because some of the early converts married into these families and remained in the district.

I have just found this letter from my father, written over 50 years ago, as follows: Mr. Jack Griffey was 9 years old when the Salvation Army came to Inverell. The first song given out in the Open-Air Meeting was:

"We are out on the ocean sailing,
Homeward bound we sweetly glide,
We are out on the ocean sailing,
To a home beyond the tide."

As an old man, he said, in his mind's eye, he could still see Captain Ford giving out the song.

The first hall they rented was later the Scout Hall. It was a few blocks up from the present Salvation Army Citadel.

Captain Ford was trying to entice people into the hall. Jack Griffey said, 'I was the first one to go through the door. Captain turned to the Lieutenant and said: We now have an audience'. Jack and Phil Hughes, later on as boys went to the Penitent form, but did not keep on. My dad later worked for Mr. Phil Hughes.

Sam had a strong, penetrating voice and could be heard a mile away at William Street when speaking at the Open-Air service in town. One shop owner paid the Salvation Army half a crown (2/6 or two shillings, sixpence) to have the weekly Open-Air Service in front of his shop.

When Sam prayed, one knew he prayed often and knew he was in touch with his Heavenly Father. He'd say, "I'm glad there is not a cloud between me and my God this morning". Those who stayed in his home would hear him praying aloud for his family and friends, before he went to work. Once, a man, very drunk, came out of the Victoria Park gardens in town, where Sam was in charge, and said, "That old man in there prayed with me."

[2] Victoria Park, Inverell

My father always told me that he retired at 70 years, but by the records he was 73. He was only retired six weeks, He didn't feel well, was in bed and they sent for a doctor. When he saw him, he said, "I think you've overdone it this time, Sam. What have you been doing?" Sam replied, "I hilled ½ an acre of potatoes with a hand hoe," He died from a heart attack shortly afterwards. (Until his death, he could touch the floor in front of his toes, with his clenched fist – that's how fit he was.)

Positions he held in the Salvation Army up till 1913: (as per the War Cry article) "I have been a local officer in the same Corps, Inverell for 2 years without a break – including Orderly and Door Sergeant, Sergeant Major, Band Sergeant,

Colour Sergeant, Recruiting Sergeant (Second commission) which I now hold. I have also worked in the Young People's Corps. I thank God I am still in possession of full salvation and after 25 years of Christian life still mean to fight till death, realizing that only to Him who is faithful till death shall the Crown of Life be given."

Norm's Stories

As told by Norm Morris

Bingara

[2] The House at Mudgee

When we were in Mudgee, we had a house cow. We lived out of town a little bit and there were quite a few vacant blocks about and an Illawarra dairy sold up, so I bought a cow. I made one mistake; I didn't hear her bellow before I took her. She was the only cow I knew that could blow herself up and bellow and bellow which made a lot of noise, but if my neighbours complained they didn't complain to me. I used to take her out of the morning, tie the chain up behind the car, and drive along and she'd walk behind the car until we got to the place where I was going to tie her up for the day. She would stand there; I would milk her and that supplied us with milk for the couple of years that we were in Mudgee.

When we left there, we were appointed to Toowong in Brisbane, which was a city church and altogether different. I had friends out at Coonabarabran, so I took her out and just let her go on their place. She was out there, with their permission of course, I think she might have had a calf while she was there. When we finally went to Inverell, I had to go and get her as I had some stock running at Warragundi, my cousin's property, so she could run with them.

To get her, Jean Helen and I took a car and a horse float down to Coonabarabran on the Saturday. On the Sunday, we put the cow in the float and drove back. I had got just through Bingara, having already blown one tire on the horse float, when I blew another one. Not wanting to proceed without a spare, I took the cow out of the trailer and took her over to tie her up to the nearest fence. I remember looking over that property and thinking that it was a nice property. There was an all-rabbit netting fence on the outside and it was tidy looking. If someone had said to me then, in five years-time you'll own that property, I'd have told them they were off their head but that was the case, we owned it in five years.

I went back to Bingara with the tires and stopped at the Bilsborough shop, owned by a young couple who were just getting started, who mended the tires. We went back, put them back on and went on our way, up through

Delungra, and back to Inverell where she joined the other cattle, I had at Warragundi.

We sold them before we went back to Bingara to live, giving us a bit of capital for the move. I'd got a loan of $600 from my father to buy about a dozen heifers. They grew up at Warragundi, and while I was working there, the overtime I did paid for the agistment of the cattle. They did very well down there on that good country. I think one of the Frame brothers ended up buying them through the sale yards.

It was a little house. The owner, having bought it to retire in, had completed some of the renovations of the toilet, shower room, all the brick foundations and a new four-car shed. One of his relatives left him quite a big property somewhere else, so he just left that to go take possession of his gift.

When we went to look at it, someone had put a cow in the backyard to eat the grass, and it had been up on the veranda leaving its calling card. My father was passing one day and went to have a look at what we were buying, he walked around the back and noticed that the back door was opened. Hearing movement inside, he started to investigate and as he got closer, the cow came out to meet him.

It was a well fenced little block, with a little orchard, I don't know whether we ever got any fruit, a piggery, lots of old stuff that we donated to the museum, and town water. It took some cleaning up, but we managed.

When we moved in, we didn't have much room really and we put up some blinds on the front veranda, so the boys could sleep out there, the girls had the front room, we had the second bedroom until we managed to complete the third bedroom which was the smallest room. This surprised my father, but I didn't tell him that the reason we picked that one was because it was the quietest, as the house was very close to the main road, and we didn't hear the trucks passing during the night. As with all families, as the children grew, and their needs changed, the sleeping arrangements were adjusted to accommodate them. Life is and has to be fluid to meet the changes it gives us.

The trucks back then weren't as powerful, so the trucks changed gears right in front of our house which covered the front facade with black smoke, as their power increased so did the distance further up the hill before they changed gears, making things quieter for us.

There were no plastic drink bottles in those days, they were all glass. Alan was keen to have a horse, and as we didn't have any spare money for it, every weekend he would strap a milk crate on the back of his bike and collect the bottles thrown out the windows by the drivers along the road. He sold them and saved his money to buy a horse. He didn't have enough, so Darrell offered him a job at shearing time to help him earn extra money. He was only there for a week and Darrell rang up and said I'd better go and get him because he was so tired that he was worried he might get sick, but he got enough money to buy a Welsh pony from a guy at Upper Horton, who had a Welsh Pony Stud, and he was selling some of them around town. I asked him what he had, and he told me that he had a Palomino stallion that would bring $20 or more if he was gelded. I told him to leave him the way he was, and I'd send someone to get him.

My father got a horse float and collected him, we called him Prince, he was beautiful, a wonderful walker, he'd keep up with the big horses all day. The boys 'broke him in' and he got on well with all the kids but never with my father, maybe he objected to being taken away from the Horton. One of his foals was the champion pony at the Bundaberg show a few years after we moved to Gympie.

While we were in the process of moving, I was busy getting stuff from Warragundi, going backwards and forwards over a period of time. I came back from one trip to find the kids upset. The white Cedar tree up the back had grubs all over it and when they had finished eating the leaves they walked off and came down, walking all around the house upsetting the kids, so we had to clean the grubs up before we could have any peace. It was our home for many years, we put on a new front and finished the back renovations using the foundations that were already there.

There was also about a 10-acre block over the road that was not part of the deal, and I rang the owner to find out how much he wanted for it, which I don't remember, but whatever it was, I didn't have that much money available. I asked if he was able to leave his money in, which he was willing to do. I then asked him how long before he wanted his money back to which he said, five years and I said, 'Oh, how about 10 years?" "Yeah, ten years, that's alright". I think he was happy to get rid of it because nobody was living on it and the neighbour's sheep were getting in under the gate. We cleared the whole debt, long before the 10 years were up.

We had a phone, (not everyone had one in those days) which I thought we were too poor to have, but my wife insisted we keep it. I came home one day for lunch from Fay's Hardware Department store where I worked, I used to ride backwards and forwards on a bike for exercise which also saved us money on petrol. I got home, and I said there's no pasteurized milk deliveries here, they used to have deliveries here when I was on the board of directors before I went to study theology, twenty years previously. My wife instructed me to ring up and find out why this was the case. I rang them to investigate, and I was told that the manager wasn't in, but George Mason was the Chairman of the Board, if I rang him, he would be able to tell me. So, I rang George, and said you fellas aren't as good as you were twenty years ago, there's no pasteurized milk down here. He said I was coming down tomorrow to get somebody to take it on, if you will take it on, I won't even bother coming, you can have all the pasteurized milk rights for Bingara. I said I don't have a cold room. He said 'Don't worry about that, we'll give you a cold room. So, we just rolled up the roller doors and pushed the cold room into one side of the four-car garage. It even had the three-point power point to run it, so we plugged it in and away we went.

We had to build it up from there, but it became a good stable business. At one stage the milk company wanted to bring the milk down and if I had some milking cows, they would take the milk back. It was a fine idea, but we needed to build a dairy, so we got a quote to build one, but we hadn't started when political deals by Neville Wran made it unprofitable and put a stop to it. I'd already bought a truck load of cows from the coast, so I turned the old killing room that was there on the property into a place to milk them. I had milking machines that I'd got off someone who had them in their shed and a diesel engine.

I got that property in an unusual way. The property, Whitlow, was about 200 acres. The block was out of town and was where I'd tied the cow to the fence on the trip back from Coonabarabran. The owner put a For Sale notice in the paper, then a little while later, another notice saying it was withdrawn. I went over to see him one day, when the idea of running a dairy was still possible.

You had this place for sale, is it still for sale?

He said, "I took it off the market but it's for sale today. I went out there this morning and my sorghum crop had been destroyed by wild pigs, the whole crop is gone. So, I put it back on market today".

"How much?"

We came to an agreement on the price, shook hands on it and I went away and got the necessary money to buy the property. We grew some wonderful crops on that place but also some rubbish ones. We had an old header, and the boys went to do some harvesting for me one day, they took the header and put it right in the middle of the thistles. They took a photo and said this is dad's good crop.

² Harvesting at Whitlow

Jean used to say to me; "if you give them a job, go away, don't worry about it, leave them to do it, and don't go there interfering with it, just let them do it", which is good advice. I used to walk around a bit in circles wondering what was going on, but that was part of growing up as a father. We were there for ten or more wonderful years.

One lady, who owned a big property on the way out of Bingara, used to come into the Hardware store, and said 'Oh, yeah, you're the man that lives in that house there just out of town, I'm amazed, every time I come past it something's happening there, something is changing, you must be good workers".

Because we couldn't sell our milk, we used to feed it to the pigs. We learnt by experience that for a litre of fresh milk we could rear a suckling pig, giving them all the protein and nourishment by adding hammer milled grain. We used to produce quite a lot of milk, 20 or 30 gallons a day. God was very good while we were there.

Once the milk run became a good business, I was able to leave my job in the hardware department and went to work doing odd jobs around town, particularly with one of the garages. I used to do some of their non-skilled work like changing springs in semi-trailers, trucks, and that sort of thing. When he was building stock yards, I'd do the pipe bending, not the technical stuff and he'd keep my vehicles on the road.

² The $300 Station Wagon

I had my father's old holden panel van, I got that off him when he bought his new Falcon station wagon. He'd got it at Warialda, I knew the agent over there and I said to him, how much for a station wagon without any trade-in and cash purchase. He gave me a very good deal. I'd bought dad's old van and used it as a back-up vehicle for the Milk run.

Bilsborough's garage said to me, "that's a very good van, it's been well cared for, and we want to buy it off you when you want to sell it". I said "OK, that'll be alright, I'll remember that." Anyway, I was nearly too slow coming to sell it. One day I said to Jean, "I think we should buy a station wagon", the kids were getting bigger. I was up in Inverell with the milk truck, which was a Datsun, and to collect the milk I had to drive past a Second-hand car yard, and in the yard was a nice-looking station wagon. I went home and said to Jean, there's a nice station wagon up there it, looks alright to me. God kind of said to me 'that's the sort of car you need' and she said, 'if that's the case, you need to go and see how much it costs.' I said "well, we've got to add up how much money we've got". We added up the money and we had just $300 to spare. Getting a Station wagon for $300, even then, didn't seem very realistic, but the next time I was up there I parked under a tree that was in front, as I was loaded with milk ready to go home. Who should walk out but a bloke who I knew from my Sunday school days, he was the salesman there and I sung out to him, "how much for the station wagon there?" He said "$300". I said "I'll buy it. I'll see you next time I'm in town". It was the easiest sale he ever made and it's probably the silliest way to buy a car, other than with God's guidance.

This was on the Wednesday, on the Thursday, I went to Bilsborough's garage, and told them that I had bought another car, the van is for sale. They said it was just as well I'd called today, because on Friday they were going to

Tamworth to buy one, but if yours is ready we won't go. So, they paid us for the van, and we had money left over to buy the station wagon, leaving us in front. That wagon served us for a long, long, time. When we bought it, we discovered it had a new engine and was more comfortable for the kids because in those days you could just pile them all in without the need for each of them having to have a seat belt.

While we were in the ministry, we had the latest model Holden station wagon and when we came to Inverell, we traded it in for some surplus money (in those days you could trade down) and bought a blue van. They used to call them 'Sinbins' because the young used to drive around in them and sleep in the back. We still had it when we moved to Bingara and when Jean's father died, we drove it up to Brisbane for the funeral. My parents came down to stay with the children. My father brought his van and did the milk run for me; it wasn't very big in those days.

We'd been there for a week or so while Jean's mother and aunty got settled in their house together, then we started home and got halfway to Ipswich when the engine blew up, went boom. I was in real trouble, so I suppose I called the RACQ and we got back to Brisbane. I rang a friend I had at Nundah, and I said to him, "you wouldn't be able to get a Milk Van for me?" He took me to the agent and when I got there, there was a yellow Datsun Milk Van specially built for milk deliveries. A fellow had bought a milk run but didn't want the truck and it was sitting there, all done up ready for sale. So, we put our gear in the milk truck and drove the Datsun back to Bingara. The vehicle hadn't been used very much and when we opened the ashtray, we found change in it, so whoever owned it had walked away pretty quick. It had back doors, side doors, and we could slide the crates backwards and forwards. We used to get big loads of milk, three days' worth, so we needed to put in heavier springs and bigger tyres on it, so that it would take the weight as we drove over the smooth roads and not so smooth ones.

[1] Telephone Booth

I remember going either to or from Inverell once when they were doing up the road. They had a side-track about a mile or two long, around the road works and I was about halfway along this track, when a milk inspector pulled me up. He wanted to know what I was up to, he asked me why I wasn't making my milk run bigger. He got a map out, pointed to a particular spot and asked me why I wasn't going to there.

What he didn't know, coming from the city, was that the only thing at that spot was an old-fashioned crossing over the Horton River. The only reason it was marked on the map was because, outside the only house there, was a telephone box that could be used if travellers got into trouble. He then proceeded to light a cigarette and it was a very hot day but when he'd finished, he just threw it away into the grass. I stomped on that pretty quickly, making sure that it was completely out and told him that if he wasn't careful, we'd be out there fighting a bushfire. I was not impressed by him. Later we used to collect the milk from Warialda, and I'd stop at Kelly's Gully, leaving milk for the store there.

That's where I saw the biggest hailstones I'd ever seen. They had a hailstorm go through there that even dinted the old-fashioned heavy iron on their roofs. They'd put some in the shop's freezer which were as big as tennis balls but all prickly, they were whopping big hailstones.

Water rises and falls with the moon, and at Kelly's Gully, there is a creek that runs through there and you can see it happen. When the moon was full you could actually see the water running down the Creek but when the moon went down the water went and just ran under the sand. Each time when the moon came full you could see the water actually come to the surface and then disappear when the moon waned.

We got the milk run to a reasonable level of profitability, and I had a chap ring me up, from Sydney, saying that he wanted to buy a Milk run in Bingara. "I take it there is only one there and I'll buy it if you will tell me how much you want for it". I think we got $12,000 for it straight off the cuff.

² Chev

I had to find something else to do, so, I did more work at the garage where I was working part-time. The owner was married to a girl from Barraba and used to go down there to his wife's people every now and again. One morning he said to me,
"Look Norm, I can get you a Chev car, a V8 Chev, it's a beautiful car."
"Yeah, that's alright but what would we have to pay for it?"
"I think you can buy it for $600."
"Good gracious how do you get that?"
"This is what's happened, the solicitor at Barraba died and in his 'Will' he left this car to be kept registered and in driving order for his wife to go to the picnic races whenever the races were on in Barraba so that she could go in dignity. Eventually the wife died, and the car is for sale. I think it needs new tyres but other than that, that's what it will cost you. I've got tyres here that are nearly new that you can have".
It was very impressive and when Jean used to drive it down shopping, they'd used say "Coo, you look as if you're driving the Queen Mary" because Jean was only a little girl really.

She went to work one morning at the school library and the gardener there, a very strict bossy sort of a man in his family, was busy mowing the lawn. He stopped the mower and said, "how's the boss this morning?" Jean said, "I'm very well, how are you?" He couldn't get back to mowing quick enough, he was quite a nice man really and Jean was very friendly with his wife who was in the kindergarten department.

My wife, Jean, was wonderful woman. She was very godly, efficient, and a great mother, but by the time she had five children around she was pretty busy. She'd always had straight hair and while she was a Salvation Army Officer, she used to do it up in a bun. She tried all sorts of different things to try and get a kink in it. Her mother, who had looked after children in a children's home always said that that there wasn't a child with hair that she couldn't get to curl. However, when her youngest girl was born, it didn't matter what she did, putting it in rags, plaits or whatever, it wouldn't even hold a wave. She told it this way, "I'm standing in front of the mirror and I'm trying to do my hair, it was a bit of a nuisance to get it nice and tidy." She only wanted to look her best. "God, now look, I don't want flash hair or anything posh, I just want it convenient so that I can get it done quickly and get on with the things I have to do for the day and within a few weeks my hair developed a kink." She had it until the day she died. She used to wash it thoroughly and do whatever ladies do to keep it in place, but she said it just happened. She didn't know if she started to eat something different but mostly it was just an answer to her prayer.

When the kids are in school, you're never quite sure what they're going to come home with. One day, Lionel came home and said to his mother, "I want to make bread". Jean had to look up bread making. We had some Bakers Meal which is a special wholemeal flour used to make bread. She made it by hand, which was quite a big job, and at that time I had a bit of stomach trouble. Lionel kept it up for about six weeks. She made buns for him to take to school, after six weeks he had enough but in that six weeks, it had cured my health problem. So, for the rest of our married life, which was quite a lot of years,

Jean made bread. She said, "I wouldn't make it except that my husband is grateful, it's good for his health, and less expensive as well". She made it by hand for about twenty-five years then they brought out Bread Makers, that was wonderful, she had just about worn it out when she went to heaven. I'm still making my own bread, but I've got to use this baker's meal. About the time Lionel decided to stop making bread for himself, he was walking along the gully, and he found a rock about the size of the buns mum made, it was even the same colour, so he brought it home. When mum put the buns out for their lunch, he put this rock in amongst them. The other kids went to get them, and here was a rock instead. His mother kept that rock as a paper weight, as a reminder of how bread making started in our house, and it's still on the office table. I still enjoy it, it's good for my health and if I eat too much commercial bread my health issues flair up again.

Pigs are very intelligent creatures and when we had the property "Whitlow" at Bingara, there was an old white sow there that for some reason had gone wild and I could never catch her. I knew she used to go around at night and get into the wheat crop and make a nuisance of herself. She had some young pigs on her so I went out one night with the rifle and stood up on a strainer post (I couldn't do that today of course). I could hear her in the wheat paddock and the young pigs sucking, over time you get to know when they're feeding their young. So, in the dark, I guessed about where she was and shot in the general direction, made contact, and killed her. We collected up some of the young ones, fed them and sold them when they were ready for market.

Pigs are unusual creatures to deal with, there was a bloke who came around, with a semi-trailer to buy pigs from different farmers and we used to take them to the semi-trailer, load them and he would then take them up to Brisbane where they were processed. On one occasion, when we were loading pigs at Warialda, we got to where we were meeting him, this day, and while we were loading the pigs, one of them got out. He ran around, near the trailer because he didn't want to go away from his mates, but nobody could catch him.

When nobody was doing any good, there was an old stockman who came up and he said, "any you fellas have a rope here?" Somebody found a rope in the back of their truck, and he whipped up a lasso and he said, "just stand back a little bit", and he lassoed this pig. I'd never seen anything like it. I was amazed at how he'd got a lasso over that pig, because he's got no neck. If I remember rightly, he got it over his head and under the first foot. While he had him tied up, somebody else got in and put him up in the semi-trailer. I was amazed at how good these fellows were in days gone by, but they had to develop those skills because that was the only way to get things done. I'd heard lots of things about good old stockman who could lasso animals, but I could never do it. We would get it over a cow's head eventually or a horse if it would stand still long enough and we had enough time.

Church Life

[2] Salvation Army Hall at Inverell

Going to the Salvation Army when I was a kid, was tiring, as there would be an Open-Air meeting somewhere first thing in the morning, then the kids would have Sunday School, while the band had prayer and practice, followed by a church service and then home for lunch. The kids would go back for a second Sunday school session and then we would attend a service again at night. My dad and I would walk to and from the night service.

I remember getting into trouble one time at Sunday School, because mum had given Hilton and I a penny each, but Hilt was given two half-pennies instead of a single coin for the offering. I put my penny in the offering and then started to cry. When asked why I was crying I told them that my brother (Hilt) was robbing God because he had only put in a half-penny instead of both the coins that mum had given him. They would sing 'Hear the pennies dropping as they fall, one by one as they fall'. A penny was a lot of money back then, you could buy an ice-cream for a penny or even a half-penny or penny chocolates wrapped in red papers.

Sometimes we would walk home after the night service with a man by the name of Ralph Jones, who lived in a house on forty acres, out past where the Soil Conservation used to be. He was a tall man with very long legs. He'd ask my dad if he would walk home with him, and dad would say, only if you don't walk too fast, as if you are going to Warialda. He'd have to slow up, he and dad would sometimes stop and talk for a while at the corner of Warialda and Auburn Vale Road. I would be so tired that I would be in tears often and think that the light on my tears was poking fun at me.

Particularly during the war, the streetlights were covered so the light only pointed straight down to the ground underneath, so there was no flair up into the sky just in case there were unfriendly airplanes in the sky above.

For a number of years, Jean and I used to go over to Cooran and do a Bible study there. There were a number of ladies from round the area who used to come. It was a good Bible study, we just discussed what God does and what His word means to us. One of the lady's daughter had left her husband and this lady used to tell me, "He's not my son-in-law anymore but he's wonderfully good to me". So, when I met him, years later, when he was doing some work for the Christian Radio Station in Gympie, I asked him; "what happened to your ex-mother-in-law?" "Oh," he said, "she died at home. They went to see her, nobody answered the door and when they got inside, there she was sitting in a lounge chair with the Bible open on her lap, reading the word of God, dead." What a wonderful way to go to heaven.

I remember one night, it was so clear, and the air was so clean up here away from the city, that as we drove over, the moonlight was so bright you could've turned the headlights off and still seen everything just like daylight. When some of the other people arrived, who had a pineapple farm at Traveston, they said; "look it was so clear you could've turned the lights off".

Just recently I had a lady ring me. My name was in the museum at Gympie. She said, "You're a minister, I have a few questions about the Bible, can you help me?" I said, "yeah I can." I forget now what the question was, but I said "you can be sure God understands and hears your prayer. That proves that God exists. Have you ever had your prayer answered?" "Oh, my," she said, "I have. I was married for a number of years and divorce wasn't in my thoughts, but she said my husband abused me that much that I eventually had to divorce him. He's very dominating and I didn't have a chance of getting anywhere to live. I was told that I would have to go and see the agent, but you'll have to have someone to say that you're being a good client to get a unit and she said I walked into the agency to see what was available, I introduced myself to the lady behind the counter and asked if they could help me with a unit. Before she could answer me, the woman in charge put her head out of an office a couple of rooms up the hall. I've got just the right unit for you, come over here and see me. She had the right unit, just what I could use but I had nothing to put in it. The first night I slept with my head on my handbag and a sheet over myself, that's all I had. Within a few weeks God provided for me all that I needed". When she heard that I was going down to Cooroy for my dentist check-up, she said to call in and see her while I was there. So, Lionel and I went in and had lunch with them. She has married again, and they seem to have a wonderful partnership. One of her sons does roof reconstruction or roof cleaning in Gympie. This just proves the wonderful stories there are about how God provides. She wasn't lazy, she used to pot plants and sell them at her gateway, in order to help keep the money coming in. Her husband was in charge of the gardens for the Cooroy Shire. So, God provided for her in a very special way.

[2] Union Church - Kilkivan

You never know where young people will go. We had friends out at a little village called Lower Wonga. When I went to Kilkivan to do church services once a month, I would call in at this place and they had a family of two or three boys and a girl or two, another family had a couple of girls and someone else had a family of five kids. This lady was a nurse and had a daughter there who used to come to Sunday school, anyway, she became a nurse like her mother and grandmother before her, nursing ran in the family. She went overseas somewhere, like young people do, to a poor country for experience, she saw how poor and needy some of these people were, when she come back to her mother, she said, "I'm so concerned about that, I'm going to become a doctor", and so she got credits for her medical work as a nurse and became a doctor. The last I heard; she was working in Alice Springs.

There is a lot of flat country between Inverell and Moree, which doesn't flood often but when it does it goes across all that country and because it's so flat,

[1] Salvation Army Cap

it walks rather than runs across it. There was a big flood up all along there, it was a very wet year and there was water everywhere. There were people marooned in all sorts of places. They sent the military in with their old military ducks that had wheels that could be let down onto the ground; if there was water, the wheels were lifted and sealed off and it would go through the water. They wanted some people to go from Inverell to Moree and see how many people they could rescue. Most people were busy, so the Salvation Army Officer said to my brother, "Here, I'll give you a Salvation Army cap, put it on your head and you can be the carer for the victims". I remember he told me that they gave him a big Thermos of either tea or coffee and for the number of drinks he gave out, it must have been like the jar of oil spoken about in 2 Kings 4:1-7, Where Elisha tells a widow, who is about to lose her sons to pay a debt, to pour oil from her jar into borrowed vessels and it keeps coming until all the vessels are full.

So, they went down to Moree towards Pallamallawa, and they came to one bridge and there on the bridge were people, snakes, pigs, animals, they're all there together at peace, one with the other. They collected up the people and gave them a cuppa and they went on down to Moree until the water subsided and then they had to come back. My brother was always amazed at how many drinks came out of that Thermos, they just seem to keep coming and coming and there was still some left in it when they had finished.

[1] Solid-Wheel Flat-bed Truck

Years ago, the Salvation Army band from Inverell went to Bingara for a tour. That was in the days before buses and flash transport. Their only transport was a truck, owned by one of the bandsmen. It was the latest model but didn't have inflated tires; they were solid rubber wheels. They left Inverell and stopped at the little villages along the way that have disappeared altogether now that railways and horse coaches are gone. It's a wonder to me that developers haven't moved in to save them for historical posterity but that's for some other fellow with more financial imagination than me. The first place they come to was Long Flat. They got out of the truck at the Post Office, which was at the top end of the village, got into their formation and played and marched all the way down the road to the school and the community memorial hall down the other end, a distance of about a kilometre.

[2] Salvation Army Band – Inverell - Wilfred Morris; Middle row, Second from left.

All the people came out to see the band, as it wasn't something you saw every day. The band got back in the truck. They travelled on the back with church seats on the truck deck with a great big piece of canvas tied over the back to try and keep the dust and dirt off them and their instruments. It would have been a very rough and dusty ride as there was no bitumen on the roads and solid tires. The next stop was at Warialda, where the show was on.

They were glad to get off the truck and shake the dust off, my dad and somebody else were walking down one of the streets towards the Presbyterian Church, which was on the other side of the Creek. As they stopped to chat to the policeman, over the Hill and down across the Creek came a family in a brand-new Model T Ford. They were funny things to drive but the driver looked pleased as punch, seemly having done away with the horse and buggy, with the wife and kids sitting beside him, however, he was driving down on the wrong side of the road, as in those days a license was easy to get. The policeman said, "Look at this, I'll stop him". He stepped out onto the road and put his hand up, but the woman had a hanky in her hand and was so excited, she waved back to him not realizing that he was trying to stop them, and they carried happily on

[2] Model T Ford

their way. The policeman went back to dad and said, "well you never know do you, what do you think of that?" but anyway there wouldn't have been any great traffic hazards in those days, particularly in a small town like Warialda.

The band did their stint at Warialda and then moved on to a place called Kelly's Gully and that was quite a village then, with at least one pub and a church. They stopped there for a short break and played a few numbers before the last leg of the journey to Bingara for the program. Fancy driving in one of those vehicles with solid tires, you couldn't say that they had independent suspension.

Such was the strength and determination of the men and women of the times.

Mr Southwell, Harry was his name, and they were quite well off. Jean hated me taking our toddler out there because everything was down low as they had no children, and it was expensive looking. My wife was always worried that our daughter might break something just by being inquisitive. They had marvellous stuff and beautiful furniture. When you went to visit, she, Mrs Southwell, treated you as if you were somebody special and she'd bring out the best china.

He was quite a character, I used to go out sometimes and help with the dipping of his few sheep and that sort of thing on the little property of about 300 acres. One of the finance people in the Salvation Army suggested that he was making a fair bit of money off his country, but because I knew what he was doing on the farm, I realised that their wealth was coming from somewhere else.

Lynden house, at Canowindra was one of the places where the Salvation Army took their children during the war out of harm's way. When we were there, they had about 50-60 girls living there, and everybody made a bit of a fuss of them. Harry said to me one day, "we spend a lot of time on Lynden House, but we don't do anything for our church. We'll have a new front put on the church." "Yeah, that's a good idea" I said. "Yes," he said, "You can cut the timber off my place. I have some nice pine trees and my wife can give a couple of pots with artificial trees in them on the condition that I have the privilege of giving the financial report when it's open". I wasn't at the opening, but I heard that Harry spoke about all the help that was given by other people and the only other thing he said was that his wife gave the pots with the artificial trees, so, nobody knew about all the other things he had done.

That's how the old people's home, that is still there in Canowindra got started. They wanted an old people's home and Harry met the commissioner of the Salvation Army and said we should have this home here. It's a nice big house and they've extended it now, no doubt, but they opened it up. He told the commissioner that he would give 1000 pounds, but they had to ask the Shire for 1000 pounds, then ask the state government for 1000 pounds, then go to the commonwealth and tell them we had 3000 pounds, we want you to match it for another 3000 pounds. They thought Harry was made of money, but he was a good businessman. Later on, I heard that his wife died, and he married again, and bought a block of ground over from Mandurama, built a house there which he lived in during his retirement. He was a very clever man. He never drove a new car in the time I knew him. He could afford one, but he always drove a second-hand car. You never knew that he had money and he did a lot of wonderful things for the people around him.

He was telling me once that you can never tell what church people get excited or have an argument about. When he was in the Methodist church in Yass, they introduced the organ. The people were so upset because they were old Methodist people from Europe and England who had always sung without music and when they got the organ, they all thought the organ was too sinful to have in the church. He was a very interesting man and a wonderful friend to me. He was a good example of Jesus' instructions in Matthew 6:2-4.

One time, when I was in Brisbane, I was selected to go to represent the Salvation Army at a chaplaincy conference. We had a woman come to give us a lecture on how to control children, and all the necessary things to make children behave properly. It was very interesting. The only thing that she didn't know was that she lived in Toowong, and so did I. The next day I was in town, and she was down there doing shopping with her lovely young son. He was in the middle of the street, down on the ground, kicking and going on because he couldn't get his own way. I thought, *oh what a wonderful demonstration of 'you can have all the theory in the world but when it comes to doing it, it's a different thing altogether'*. She never knew I saw her and what was going on, or that I'd been one of her students the day before. It just shows, it is one thing to be full of knowledge and not wisdom; it's another thing to apply it.

[1] Kerosene Lantern

Inkie MacIntosh was the brother of Margie MacIntosh and was a councillor on the Kilkivan Shire. He came in from Widgee to the Gympie Presbyterian church one Sunday, which was a fair way to drive, then the next Sunday he was back. I said, 'we've seen you two Sundays in a row, Inkie, how come? "Yeah," he said, "I came in last Sunday to ask God for some rain on some improvement pasture seed I'd just planted, and I got some very good rain, so I came back today to thank him for it." That was the sort of character the MacIntosh's were.

A few years afterwards there was a dry spell, so the shire called for a prayer meeting out at Widgee for some rain. Inkie had died by this time. A number of ministers were asked to speak and pray at this function. I rang his wife and asked for permission to tell the story and she said, "that's quite alright you can do that", so I told the story. Afterwards, I was talking to the Anglican man who was filling in at Gympie from Toowoomba. I told him that I knew something of the good work the Anglicans carried out in the Gulf country in such places such as the Mitchell River and Edward River Missions. I told him about my stay with Father Brown who was at Edward River Mission, when I was younger. "He was a remarkable man", I said, "living in a Pandanus palm hut, his only convenience a kerosene light".

'Oh, that would be the same Father Brown who was in his 90s, living in the Retirement village at Toowoomba, and has not long passed away".

When I was visiting him, the natives were straight out of the bush with bones in their noses, their earlobes were pulled right down so they came down right down the side of their face and the men had scars all down their chest and over their stomachs which they had rubbed Ashes into to make them look bigger, to make them look more manly, I'm not sure if some of them didn't have their front teeth knocked out as well.

I came down after the wet season, to the Mission on the Bishop's launch, which brought his supply of a 44-gallon drum of lighting kerosene. The tides were long, so they tipped it over the side, and it floated into the shore on the incoming tide, and they rolled it up to Father Brown's hut. He must have had a great love for the natives to live there all those years, telling them about Jesus and what God can do for them. He loaned me a book to read 'The Stone Age men of Today' by JRB Love, which is now a very famous book and considered one of the great authorities on the early aboriginals and their behaviour in the North of Australia.

After my wife was killed in a car accident and I was home under transitional care for a few months, I rang a friend of mine and said, "I wonder, can you find out where the chaplain for the woman's security jail is?" He rang around, and after a few days he rang back telling me that he'd found where the chaplain lived. She was the wife of the Home Missionary at Maleny. When I rang him, I said, "this is Norman Morris, you wouldn't know me but I'm inquiring about the chaplain for the Women's Prison and wondering whether she could make contact with the lady that caused the accident." He said "yeah, I know you. You did the services at Margie MacIntosh's at Widgee, 32 years ago and I'd never heard a Presbyterian minister preach about the love of God and the power of Jesus Christ like you did and because of that, I became a Home Missionary in the Presbyterian Church. My first wife died, I'm married again, and my second wife is the chaplain of the jail".

The MacIntoshes were one of the original families to settle at Widgee. In her home, a big old Queenslander, Margie built a Chapel on one of the side verandas, it was the easiest service I ever did because I'd go out and do Religious Instruction and Maggie arranged the service for the same day and everybody would turn up. It was a great time in the country town of Widgee. On one occasion, concerned about religious instruction, I asked Margie, "do you think one of the ladies here would do it for me and save me having to come out to do it every week?" She said, "See that lady over there, she'd be the first one to ask, then see that lady over there she'd be the next one." So, I spoke to the first lady, and she said she couldn't do it as her husband wasn't into Christianity and he only let's her come to the service because it's Margie's place so she couldn't do it. I told her that's alright, so I went to the next lady and asked her about doing religious instruction she said no, she had too much on. I said, "Oh yeah, OK that's alright".

I used to go out there one day during the week, after religious instruction, visiting. Jean would pack me some lunch. I'd do religious instruction and then I'd visit around the neighbours and different people that came to the church at Margie's. I eventually got to Jeanette Elliott's place, they were up at Little Widgee, and had built a nice big home there where they bred Australian Stock horses as well as turning off beef cattle. They had all their furniture made of Cedar from their previous property at 1770. It was beautiful furniture.

John, her husband, was a very good organizer and did very well at whatever he did. I knocked on the door, she answered it and said, 'I know what you're here for, you're going to try and persuade me to do religious instruction". I said, "no, you said you couldn't do it, that was enough". "Oh", she said, "God's given me no peace since you asked if I could do it. How do I go about it?" I said "well, I'll show you how I do it, but you need to do it your way; I'll give you the material". She said, "Oh, yeah, that's OK then".

Their previous property was a long way out of town, and she'd home schooled her two boys, so she had a good idea about teaching herself. She came on the first day at school and she was so pleased with it she said, "I can do that". She was wonderful with the kids and the kids loved her. When they got through the end of primary school and going to high school in Gympie, Jeanette gave every child a Bible, so they all had a Bible of their own to take home. She was wonderful in that way.

Her husband John suffered from an aneurysm, they got to him in time and patched it, twice. He was one of the few fellows to survived it.

When he had his first attack, they didn't expect him to live but he said afterwards that he had been up to the pearly gates and said everything is light and beautiful up there, I really didn't want to come back. He wrote some of his experiences out and gave them to me. He was very active and used to do cattle drafting on his Australian stock horses. His blood line of horses was quite famous, bringing big money, they were all high quality, sought after stock.

Their home had some bedrooms down the other end where young people could stay. On the night that John went home to Heaven, they had a young couple staying who John was counselling on how to keep their marriage together; be kind to one another, it's a partnership, no one is a boss over the other. After he talked to them for a while, they all went off to bed and during the night John had his final attack. Jeanette knew it was possible for John to not survive this time said to him, "just follow the lights, just like you did before" and she said he died peacefully. She rang the undertaker and they asked if she was alright and if she wanted them to come out immediately. She said to just leave it till morning and she laid John out in the correct way because she had been a nurse and had travelled around the world in her single days. She rang her son in Hong Kong, who was a Pilot in Cathay Pacific Airlines. She told him that she didn't know how to tell the young couple who were staying with them that John had died during the night. He said, "Mum, stand up straight, walk down that corridor and just tell them", so that's what she did.

As it happened, I was out with Alan, our oldest boy, we were going out to the other side of Wandoan to kill a beast and bring the meat back in the mobile freezer.

When I got there, the lady came out and said, "If you're Norm, you're wanted on the phone". When I got on to it, Jeanette told me John had died and I want you to do the funeral. In those days, Gympie didn't have a crematorium and so we had to go down to Buderim for the cremation and they took a double time slot because it would be a very big funeral. We killed the beast, made our way back to Mt Gravatt, where Alan was living at the time, I drove to Gympie, turned around and drove down very early the next morning to Buderim to do the service there.

That was the first time I saw a computer laptop, John's son had one of the latest things from Hong Kong, he was there, so we sorted out the service. The Cremation took place according to what family wanted and particularly Jeanette as she was Queen of her family in those days. She stayed on at Little Widgee for quite a good while and did the school and got known as the Mother Teresa of Widgee, as when anybody got into trouble or had some crisis in the family, Jeanette continued to guide and direct them in what should be done, giving comfort or counsel or whatever she could. Sadly, she couldn't keep up with the farm and somebody from the Arab countries finished up buying it.

My mother and father used to tell me that they had a minister at their church who had been a Stockman in the days before fences. They were called shepherds and they would look after the sheep during the day and at night they would put them in a pen to keep them away from the dingos and foxes. Because there were no fences, they had to use their lassos to catch some of the animals that decided to stray.

This particular minister had been a Jackaroo and was very good with the lasso, so at church picnics he'd get the kids to run in a circle round him and then he'd lasso their foot as it came up. He was that clever.

One of the other things they used to do at what were called *bush picnics* was "Catch the Greasy Pig". They would rub a pig with fat, let the pig run around, and everyone would chase it and try to catch it. There would be a prize for the person who eventually managed to catch it.

Family

Before Jean and I were married we used to go down to Redcliffe. She had two uncles there, one of which was blind. While he and his father were working on the railway line between Rockhampton and Longreach they were blasting and one didn't go off right, one of his sons got caught, getting gravel in his eyes. They went straight to the nearest doctor, who was so drunk he couldn't do anything, so they had to go all the way to Rockhampton. When they got to Rockhampton it was too late, so they had to move in a hurry to see if they could have something done in Brisbane but there was nothing they could do, and he was blind for the rest of his life.

He got married and they lived on the main drive down to Redcliffe. He worked as the quality control inspector of the baskets and things that the blind people made in Brisbane. He wrote a hymn, which is here somewhere in our things that are stored away. He was very pleased with Jean because she used to write him poems and write back and forth to him and we used to go there to see them. It was one of those sad things that probably wouldn't happen today but back then they happened, and people had to make the best of it. His brother lived nearby. Their surname was Gunders, he was a good builder and was the Gunders who built a lot of a Methodist churches around Brisbane, while he was in the ministry.

He had a son, who was a pilot during WWII, one of the few pilots who did eleven flights over Germany and came back, not many people got past three, but he did, and he was a Methodist minister too. I met him when Jean lived at Laidley, and I went up to see her and stayed at his place one night. One of their relations has been a United Church minister in Bowen up near where my daughter is working.

Grandfather Gunders, he was the father of all these wonderful men and women who helped to make Australia great. He came from Norway and Sweden, and they wanted him to stay in Sweden. He said, "No, I wanna get away from here altogether from me relations," and he came out to Australia on a ship that sailed around Cape Horn where all those storms happen. When he got to Australia, he did all sorts of things, building and so forth. That's where his son who built the Methodist churches learnt his trade. His biggest problem was that he had gold fever, he'd would have liked to have found a gold pot. Some of his children were born in Charters Towers because he was up there looking for gold, but I don't think he ever found anything substantial to pass on to his family.

When he retired, he lived at Darra, near Oxley, in Brisbane. Jean's family, when she was a kid, would go out to his place. He had a humpy there and they used to play in the gravel pits that were around there. When you haven't got TV, kids initiative is much better because they have to make their own fun. They enjoyed their time up at grandfather's place. He lived there until he was in his eighties. He used the ride a push bike from there to Wynnum which helped him to keep fit.

[2] Kings Plains Homestead

Kings Plains Homestead: Aunty Alice, that's Grandfather Dean's sister, worked there as a housekeeper when the original Viver's family owned it. I went to school with the Viver boys. They used to come down to the high school at Inverell. It's still there in operation, folk I know have been there to stay at the place. There were three children in the Deans family, Joe, seven years later, Bob, and then after another seven years Alice arrived.

She lived on the property until she eventually retired and then went into a home, owned by some of the family's relations that were 'Brethren' people. The property was a substantial station in days gone by and a place where the wealthier people in that area lived and moved. It was quite some place up towards Glen Innes.

[2] Alice Deans

In the days before the war, Joe had a Bakers shop in Coonabarabran, Bob worked for him before he went to the war and Bob's name is on the War Memorial in the main street there in Coonabarabran. When I was at

[2] War Memorial at Coonabarabran, and close-up view showing Robert Deans.

Coonabarabran years ago, visiting around the area as a Salvation Army Officer, a lady said to me: I knew a fellow that belonged to your religion once, and I was sweet on him when he went to war. I asked her what his name was. She told me his name was Robert Deans, he went to the war, and she never heard any more about him, whether he came back or what happened to him. I replied, "well, I can tell you something about him. He stopped a bullet in France, came back to Australia and he wasn't married until he was in his 40s. I'm married to his youngest daughter". She said, "I never heard anything, and life had to go on". She just assumed that he had gone off and got killed or something during the war. There would have been a lot of people like that, and life had to go on and I guess she married someone else then and made the best of life.

It goes to show how God's plans for our lives differ from our own, how many wonderful people would not be here except that the circumstances of two people had changed.

[2] Deans' Family
L-R: Jean, Ron, Joan, Emily, Robert (Bob)

[2] Uncle Will Piggot

When I was about thirteen or fourteen, I bought a cow off my Uncle Will Piggot when they sold up their dairy herd. Everyone wanted black Jersey cows and there were a number of silver ones in the sale. I purchased one for eight pound ten shillings. We kept her for a period of time, milking her, and when Uncle Tom Piggot, Will's brother, retired to the Inverell district, he bought a house and block at Gilgai, and needed a cow. So, I sold the one that I had purchased from Will Piggot's herd for ten pounds including delivery. This would have been my first financial venture.

When we first moved to Dunreath, the back paddocks were part of the Long Plain region. The early farmers must have been very conscientious, because they had picked up all the stones, and put them into big heaps, like little hills. When we were kids, we used to go out chasing rabbits that lived in amongst these piles of rocks. We'd pull rocks out to find them. I saw a snake swallow a rat for the first time while we were on one such ramble.

One time, I accidently hit my cousin and friend, Ralph Brown's finger with a large rock. He probably still has a deformed fingernail because of it and has reminded me of his painful experience occasionally. Boys will be boys, and sometimes the consequences of their antics leave permanent reminders.

At one time when they were paving the highways, the roads department used the rocks for the bitumen after crushing them.

I was always interested in farming, cows, and animals but my brother was a born mechanic, he couldn't help himself, he wanted to know how things worked. It's no wonder he became a good pilot. He worked, when he left school, at Wilkinson garage as an apprentice mechanic. Billy Wilkins was a good mechanic who kept a lot of vehicles, including tractors, going during the war. It was always a busy place, as they were the Chrysler and Nuffield Agents and because they were so good at their job, the several mechanics were always flat out.

When Hilton first started working there, he rode his bike and then managed to get a Woolsey 4-cylinder utility that would often break down, so some nights he would be late home because he'd had to get the car going again. However, one night after he'd been working there for a year or two, it came around to 10:00 o'clock and he wasn't home yet. We had a phone, so my mother rang up Wilkins and asked if they had seen Hilton there that day. Whoever answered the phone said, 'no, he's never been here' and she nearly dropped the phone. Eventually someone realized who she was talking about, 'oh," they said "you're talking about Sambo, is his name Hilton? We didn't know that was his name. When he came to work, he never told us his first name was Hilton, then we christened him Sambo and he's been Sambo ever since. He's alright, we can see his legs sticking out from under a car there somewhere. He's still working on it.' To my mother's relief he turned up not long afterwards.

They used to play tricks on the new staff, but they couldn't get away with that on Hilton because he knew too much when he went to work and understood motorcars. Often, they would send a boy, fresh out of school, up to one of the other workshops to get a can of fresh air. When they'd get there, they'd say "oh, we just run out of that" and send them to another garage and they would sometime visit two or three venues before they realised that they were being played.

I had my first lesson in being careful with my money, when I was a kid. My parents gave me sixpence one year to go to the show. That was a lot of money in those days as things were tough during the depression. I went to a side-show bloke, I put up three pence to throw a die, but he told me that if I'd just been a little better, I'd have won a watch, which I thought would be the most wonderful thing, so I had another go, after only receiving three dud pencils that kept breaking when you tried to sharpen them. Again, I was told that if I had been a bit better, I'd have managed to get that watch. I made up my mind there and then that no side-show man would get any more of my money. If I went to the show after that, I would buy my sisters an ice-cream or some other sort of food, but I never spent money at the side-shows ever again.

These days I'm not quite sure what a woman's skills have to be, to be a wife, mother, and a housekeeper but they seem to be entirely different to what my grandmother needed. I remember when I was young, I used to go across to her house, they lived about a mile and a quarter away from where I lived, on my three-Wheeler bike. I used to ride down, and I'd be out of sight for quite a while, and then I'd go across what we called the black flat and my mother could then see me riding my Three-Wheeler bike. People would be horrified today if children that young, two or three years of age, were allowed to do such a thing. I'd ride across there and up William Street, and I'd pull into Grandma's house. I spent a lot of time with her.

[1] Tricycle

I remember asking her once what was wrong with her fingernails, because she had very hard, coarse looking fingernails. She said that it was from when she had to make soap. When she was first married, soap was made out of fat and caustic soda. The caustic soda ruined them, so the cleanliness of the family cost grandmother the quality of her fingernails. Now they paint them, and you wouldn't know what's underneath but in those days that was part of the price of being a quality housekeeper or mother.

Of course, you have to have wheat to have bread flour, and years ago they wouldn't try to grow wheat West of Goondiwindi in Queensland. It was just not done. My uncle Tom Gray was a very adventurous sort of a fella and he reckoned you should be able to grow it west of Goondiwindi, so he leased a block of land, of some hundreds of acres, and pushed up the sticks, stumps, and logs. His two boys, Lionel and Rod, used to go out and do the farming but, in those days, it was pretty primitive and to get enough power they put two Case tractors together. They took the front wheels off one tractor, hitched it to the second and rewired the controls so they could be operated by the driver and that's how they got into the big-time tractors.

The grazers around there thought he was off his head, he's got no idea what should happen but, one year in particular, he had a good crop, harvested by a nephew with a new autoheader that could cut fourteen feet at a time, it was hot dry weather so they could harvest day and night and they did. His neighbours would fly over his place every morning to check on how this funny wheat farmer was getting on and were amazed.

Of course, today, this is normal farming practice only they use bigger harvesters and it's put straight into the trucks instead of bags, but they still don't stop and there are thousands of acres of wheat grown out that way now, but the first wheat was grown by Tom Gray.

In those days, wheat had to go into a bag and when I worked at Crooble, they had a twelve-foot cut autoheader, with steel wheels and a platform fastened to the side and you had to sew the bag up standing on the platform while it moved along, that was my job. The bag had to be sewn tight enough to have one hundred and sixty-eight pound or more in it, the vibration of the header did help to shake it down into the bag. They were stacked in one corner

[1] Steel-Wheeled Tractor

of the platform and every so often, I had what they called the dump line, you'd flip up a rail holding the bags and they all fell off into the dump line and had to be picked up later. During my time there they didn't grow big lots of wheat; they were down to five or six hundred acres of wheat where previously they used to grow four thousand acres. It was loaded onto a truck, taken to the siding to be stacked by the 'wheat lumpers' because in those days there was no bulk handling, it was all stacked up there to be shipped by train, on timber railway jinkers. Two Maori men came over every year, one was a big thick-set fellow and the other one was tall and skinny. They bought their wives and families and had good tents with wooden floors, they set up and lived there until the season was over. To save time, and waiting in line to be unloaded, the men at Crooble went to the 'wheat lumpers' and told them that they would load them straight onto the timber jinkers but they could count the bags and add them to their tally, something they were very happy about. One day we loaded 600 bags for the day. Off the ground to the truck then at the railway restack them again, I remember feeling very tired that night, considering the bags were heavier than I was, it's no wonder.

This is one of the incidents that happened while I was there that really startled me. There was a chap working on one of the trucks in line and he was wearing shorts. He had a big scar from his hip right down to his knee, a very big wide scar. Cheeky me, I was only young, lacking wisdom, and discretion, said, "How did you get that scar?"

He looked at me and said, "Oh I've got a German bone in there, not my own".

"You've got a German bone; how did you get that?"

He said that, during the war, in Italy if I recall correctly, he got hit and smashed with a bullet and broke that bone that runs from your hip to the knee and taken prisoner. He said "I was lying there in the hospital in agony and next to me was a German who was dying from other wounds as well. The doctors came in and said, we'll see what we can do. They took the bone out of the German that was dying and put it into my leg". They must have done a good job because he was there working on a wheat truck. Sometime afterwards I thought, he was pulling my leg. I was being cheeky, and he pulled my leg. Years later when my wife had to have a hip replacement, I was talking to the surgeon, when we'd finished the consultation, I said to him, "can we have a change of subject?" He said, "by all means", and I told him what happened in the wheat lumping days and this fella who claimed he had a German bone in him, that's incredible because that was before penicillin. "yeah, I think you can believe him" he said, "we accept that during the war there was a lot of experimenting done and they must have got it right, because he didn't get an infection."

[2] Farming at Crooble

In the days when Crooble planted big lots of wheat, one of their paddocks was 1100 acres. There were no big tractors like there are today. They were all steel wheels, or crawler type tracks, Crooble had two, a WD40 and a Track D40. The Track D40 could pull a bit more weight but was slower. They had two combine drills for wheat behind it and they used to start off around this paddock, but it was so big that the driver had to take morning tea with him to have halfway round. Thousands and thousands of tons of wheat came off Crooble station. Mr Uebergang was telling me once that they had to burn the stubble in a paddock because the stubble was so thick, they couldn't work it in. We had sheep running on, so we mustered them all, then tied a burning tube to some vehicle that could travel very fast around the paddock so that it wouldn't get away. The fire burnt fiercely and when it finished, they discovered that they had missed two sheep, but the fire was so fast that it didn't burn them except their feet because they had laid down.

When I lived at Crooble, my accommodation was in the shearing quarters, my toilet, like most people, was what they called a long drop variety. The toilet was built over a very deep hole, I don't know how deep it was, but it had been in use for a long time, and it was still a long way to the bottom, where there lived a black snake, which was there the whole time I was living there. What a place for a snake to live, you could see him, but he couldn't get out, because it was too steep and too far down.

My sister's husband and his people grew wheat around North Star and once, when the parents were burning the stubble, the wind changed direction, driving the fire back the other way, killing them. They had six or seven children who had to be reared by other family members. A tragedy that affected them all, but they overcame their anguish and were successful adults.

When we were dairy farming at Goomong Road, I was getting behind with the sowing of the feed for the cattle, so one morning I told God that I just needed someone who could drive a tractor. I didn't like letting others near the cows in case something happened to the stock which are harder to replace. When I came home that evening, Jean said to me "I had a fellow call in today, who wants to milk cows" I said "He wants to milk cows? Did you get his phone number?" I rang him up and said, "You really want to milk cows?" "Yeah", he said, "I want to milk cows. I haven't milked cows for a long time, and I want to milk cows". By that time, we had the herringbone system working well, so, I said come over and have a try. He came over and he just loved the cows, and he was the best dairyman I had. He'd told his wife that he was going to get a job milking cows and his wife had told him not to be so silly. He was so good, that we were able to take a holiday, his wife came and lived in our house and looked after him.

There was one funny incident while he was working with us. We were number recording with Jean, and I said to Alf, go and get that cow with the udder. Jean couldn't believe that with eighty black and white cows in the yard, all with udders I'd asked this guy to get the cow with the udder, but he knew which animal I was talking about and brought her in for us.

[2] Nathan and Christine Morris

My grandson, before he got married, was working around Normanton, in the north of Queensland. They would round up Brahman cattle. The biggest load they sent away was sixteen road trains. The final load of cattle ended up coming down to the abattoirs in Gympie. One day, he got bumped which gave him a concussion and landed him in the Normanton hospital. His sister (a medical professional) rang up to check on him, only to discover that they weren't taking it very seriously. His father then rang the property owner, to inform him that his great worker didn't appear to be getting satisfactory treatment and should have been in a bigger hospital like Mt Isa. The owner managed to get him to Mt Isa by getting in touch with the Royal Flying Doctor Service, to which he contributed each year, and they collected my grandson and flew him to Mt Isa where he was able to recover faster.

Being accountable to someone, from time to time can be a good thing for all of us, especially if we are inclined to get a little sluggish.

² 'Uplands' Nullamanna

My dad used to go out to the Gray's property, he was friends with Tom and Ralph, long before he started courting my mother. The original Uplands was pretty dry, and in order to get water they had to place a tank, often a big square ship tank, on a large fork shaped log and the horse would pull it down to the spring on the neighbouring property, where it would be filled up using buckets and dragged back to the house so there would be water for housework, laundry, and even the dairy. When they purchased this property, it meant that they had permanent water.

In a good season, there was a couple of dams that held good water, and the boys would get me to chase the ducks off one dam so they could shoot them when they landed on the other one.

Grandma Gray had been to Nullamanna to do Sunday School or something, and on her way home discovered that the boys had been swimming in the dam, no doubt they had done so naked or in the barest underclothes, which would have to dry before they put their other clothes on. However, she sent my father home, with instructions that he was never to return to the Gray home. It took years for my mother to discover that the real reason for his banishment was because he had acquired some tobacco from one of the workmen and they were experimenting with smokes, and not related to swimming in the dam in a state of undress. Grandma Gray was very strict, but they had to be tough to survive.

Using a farmer's paddock for travelling teams along the stock routes was frowned upon but still done, particularly if there was good feed and a fair chance that they wouldn't get caught during the night. It happened once at the Gray's place, the drovers would travel along the stock routes with teams of horses and the stock camps were usually where there was water for the horses. They had their suspicions that one drover was putting his whole team in a good paddock they had. So, Grandfather Gray said to his son, Tom, 'let's go down there early in the morning to catch him getting his team out". Grandfather Gray took his shotgun with him, just in order to give the fellow a fright. Tom told me it was really funny, because when the bloke turned up, he had a dog with him, and the dog came along and sniffed the end of the shotgun, we didn't move while the dog sniffed the gun, but the idea was to stop the fellow from making a habit of spelling his team in our paddock.

The Gray bothers started the Inverell abattoirs down on the Ashford Road before it was moved to its current location. They were only getting one shilling a head for sheep so they decided to kill their own, there was an old-fashioned abattoir there, so they got a butcher's cart and they travelled around town with dressed (killed, skinned, and gutted) sheep on the back, and they pulled up outside the houses and if you wanted a leg of lamb, they would cut it for you right there, causing a row amongst the butchers in town because they were taking their customers and they complained about how unhygienic it was. Later they sent meat over to the coast, such were the small beginnings of our town's biggest employer.

When the Gray brothers, Tom and Ralph, started the abattoirs out on the Ashford Road, they had a fellow looking after the pigs that they kept out there ready for slaughter. White pigs weren't seen much about in those days, but I was out there one day, and I saw that they had a big white sow.
"Oh, you've got a white sow", I said.
"Yes, we call her ink."

"Why do you call her ink?"
"Because she runs in and out of the pen."

2 Cow with twin Calves at William Street

My grandma Morris lived over on William St for a long time. She lived there in the days before cement, these early people were very resourceful. In the horse stable, so it didn't get all muddy and boggy when it rained, they had wide timber planks laid side by side so the horse could stand on the planks instead of dirt, and they did the same where the buggy or the sulky was kept, so the floor was solid all the time. It was done by cutting big trees that gave you planks eighteen inches across or perhaps two foot across. These were hand split with sledgehammer and wedges.

1 Wedges

She was still living in William St when I had the milk run, so after I finished work on Mother's Day, I went to the market garden, they didn't have florist shops back then, they grew all sorts of vegetables and flowers and bought her a large bunch of Chrysanthemums, she was a wonderfully patient old grandmother to me. I would often go over and pray and read the Bible for her. She wanted me to read the Salvation Army Psalm, I didn't know there was such a Psalm. She told me to read Psalm 150 and sure enough it, says: '

Praise Yah!
  Praise God in his sanctuary!
  Praise him in his heavens for his acts of power!
[2] Praise him for his mighty acts!
  Praise him according to his excellent greatness!
[3] Praise him with the sounding of the trumpet!
  Praise him with harp and lyre!
[4] Praise him with tambourine and dancing!
  Praise him with stringed instruments and flute!
[5] Praise him with loud cymbals!

Praise him with resounding cymbals!
⁶ Let everything that has breath praise Yah!
   Praise Yah!

Eventually she sold William St because she couldn't keep up the maintenance of the large block and moved up into Brae Street, opposite where mum and dad lived, she and aunty Dot lived there for a number of years. She lived well into her eighties but went to Heaven after having a fall, shattering her hip and, I've just realized after reading some of my mother's letters, that she also got the mumps when she went into hospital.

My grandma Gray was a big-hearted woman, there was mother and daughter there who lived nearby. I forget what happened that left them without anywhere to live, but Grandma Gray organized Grandfather Gray to build a hut for them, down the yard where they lived at Uplands. The daughter used to look after her mother, or mother looked after daughter, or maybe they just looked after each other.

They used our washhouse to do their washing and my mother tells of how one day the wind was blowing hard, which it quite often did, and the daughter was trying to hang some sheets on the clothesline, it was one of those old-fashioned ones with a stick prop in the middle and the wind was making it very hard. Finally, the daughter stood back and said, "the Devils in the sheets I can't do anything with them." In those days, it was the personal initiative of people, like the Gray's, who stepped in to give kindness and care to so many people who fell on hard times, so they had some hope in their hopeless situations.

Stealing isn't anything new, it has always been around. Some years ago, when we were on the property at Goomong, on the Mary River, when I was raising stud Friesian cattle, we had six head disappear, I couldn't prove they had been stolen but, because they were stud cattle, they were all photographed to go with their stud papers and registered number. This prevented arguments about their pedigree. I brought the rest of them in and branded their stud number on the other side of the regular brand. I knew that if they went missing again, they could be traced.

Sure enough, about a year later, another seven of these cattle disappeared and I knew I could prove they were mine this time. I rang the stock squad, the ones that go around investigating stock theft. When they turned up, talk about big policemen, three big fellows, I explained what I'd done. They said, 'We'll go around and have a look', for a week or fortnight they went round the properties and then they came back and informed me that they haven't found them but in between times the neighbours were ringing up and saying, "where are your stock? We are under suspicion because we join your place". I told them what I had done. Another neighbour said that they would be very hot property because of how I had made sure they could be identified. So, there was a little excitement in the neighbourhood because Morris' cattle had disappeared. The Police officers paid us another visit and said, "we can't find them, in actual fact, but just keep us posted."

After they left our district, four of the seven cows that had disappeared turned up in the back paddock. I rang the Stock Squad and told them that four of them were back. He asked me if I found them on the road. I said, "no, they weren't on the road, they were back in the paddock where they came from". He told me that was unusual, that often after they have visited places the cattle are put out on the road in the hope that they will go home. One cow had a bullet hole through her ear so whether someone had tried to shoot her for meat, and she moved her head at the wrong time we will never know for sure.

My aunty Joy was the quiet one in our family, she married Hugh Fuller, he was the one that had the water put in his lantern, but Joy was very quiet and placid. She did the housework and cooking on her own, in those days, it was a big job because it wasn't only for the family but the workmen they employed to look after all the animals. It seemed that someone wasn't looking after the pigs properly and an old boar pig kept coming up poking around the house trying to find something to eat and making a nuisance of himself. So, Joy went out the back with a saucepan of hot water and threw it on him. Everybody was amazed that she'd be so ruthless, she must have been very frustrated. They say pigs are very intelligent and we never heard about him coming back again. Being scolded once must have been enough, they usually only scold them when they are taking the hair off them when they kill them.

After Aunty Joy and Uncle Hugh were married and they were living in Grafton, he was responsible for the railway but when the war came, they were told that if they had relatives inland, they'd better go up and stay with them. So, for some months, Joy, George, the oldest boy and Beryl, whose twin had died and was very quiet like her mother, came and lived on our front veranda and front room. The front room had double doors that opened out on to the veranda. Mum and dad got some roll-up striped canvas blinds to give them some protection. It would have been very difficult, but mum said, the war was on, and we had to help each other as much as possible. They lived there until ultimately Uncle Huey was appointed to the railway in Inverell and they bought a house in Chester St. I think. Uncle Huey was always great thrifty man like Joy, they were a wonderful couple together. Everybody was always amazed at how they got to have such a lively boy like George. Uncle Huey was great on gardening, he had a good garden of lettuce and vegetables of all sorts. He came home from work one day and they're all gone. He said to Joy, "Where are all the vegetables gone?" They discovered that George had got his billy cart, picked them all and gone down the street, going door to door selling them. So, George was in pocket, even if his parents were without their vegetables.

[2] George Fuller

George always did, and he still does, things with great enthusiasm. Some of his children are remarkable too, he had a girl who had asthma problems like grandfather Gray, and she had a son. My daughter was in Inverell once and she saw this young fellow there and she said to herself, where on earth have, I seen that nervous activity before and sure enough she was in another store, the same fellow was there. She made some inquiries and sure enough he turned out be George Fuller's grandson. He was as hoppy as his grandfather, getting things done; so, it must be genetic.

[1] [Left]
Wall covered in newspaper.

[2] [Right]
Dot and her children.

One day, Ralph Gray was about to come to town, but before he left, he was inspired to take Dot O'Brien a billy of milk, and a dozen eggs as he'd heard that she was living in a small place back in Inverell. When he found her, he discovered that she was living in a drafty old stable. She was an independent person and a wonderful seamstress, but things had gone haywire with her marriage, and she had returned to Inverell with her two children, Max and Muriel. Ralph told my mother about Dot's situation, and so the next day, mum went to visit Dot, with Hilton in the pram and me walking beside it, loaded up with newspaper, flour, and water. They made flour and water paste and plastered over the cracks of the planks on the stable wall, to help make it warmer to live in. No doubt she took over some meals as well. She raised her family as a single mum, with the support of her family and did very well for herself. In her seventies she remarried, and they lived in Delungra and would come and visit us sometimes in Bingara and we had some wonderful fun nights with them.

[2] Steel-Wheeled Tractor

Today, with these modern farming machines, it doesn't seem much. When we went farming the war was on. The Fordson tractor was a pre-war Kerosene model. You had to start it on petrol. Then when the hot box got hot enough, you turned it over to run on kerosene. They were slow, in first gear you would be going less than one mile an hour, second gear, a bit over one mile an hour, top gear, (there were only three), was about three miles an hour but most of your work was done in second gear. You'd be driving around in the cold weather around Inverell, the wind would be blowing, and you'd go down one side, the wind would be nice and warm as it blew into your face because it was off the hotbox and then you'd turn around and go down the other side, there would be wind but no heat, after a couple of days the skin would be peeling off your face. If I wanted to work at night, I used to have a lantern hung on the front so I could follow the last plough furrow. It was an exercise in physical endurance but much quicker and more economic than having eight horses around and feeding them. The seat was a steel one on a bouncy piece of steel to allow for some movement, the wheels were steel, with what we called "big steel spuds" on them to help grip the ground covered by big protective mudguards. If you went over the road, you had to be very careful otherwise you could rip up the road.

When the war was over, we bought a new tractor for 600 pounds. It was a wonder! It had a big battery in the front, a self-starter, a better clutch and all sort of things and lights, big lights! I don't know where they came from, but you could see way ahead. It was wonderful! You can do twenty acres in less than one day. I suppose the trouble was we were inclined to travel too fast then and that didn't do the soil much good. It was a wonderful improvement but even then, there was no air conditioning like they have today, you just sat out in the open. Later on, the Massey Ferguson and others had to have roll bars on them, but I've never had a tractor with air conditioning. The only air conditioning I got was when I retired and got a comfortable car.

[1] Wooden Highchair

When I was a very young child, like most children, I had a highchair. In those days there was no plastic, so it was all made of wood. Like lots of children I didn't like my crusts. Even though I was very young, I struck on the idea that if I stuck them under the wooden table in front of me, I wouldn't have to eat them. Eventually my parents woke up to what I was doing and what amazes me is that they said "Oh, isn't he clever" they didn't say 'isn't he born a natural liar and corrupt' because that's what I was. You haven't got to teach your child how to be, say, or do something wrong, it's just natural.

I have one cousin older than me, and he came to see me when I was first born and because I was born in February, the weather would have been hot and there was no air conditioning available, I would have been in just a nappy. He turned to his father and said, "Oh dad, he's just like a skinned rabbit".

[1] The Red Book

When I was growing up, I remember my parents had what they called a "Red Scripture Book". It was part of the training of the Salvation Army. When people got married and were setting out, they were given this book to read so that they were aware of the scriptures and how they relate to life. It had a scripture for breakfast, a short one for lunchtime, and one for after dinner. Now that was fine when my father worked in town and had his shop as he had to be at work at 8:00 o'clock. He'd get up early, milked the cow and did whatever jobs needed to be carried out and did the reading before he headed off to work. If he came home for lunch, they would have a quick read before he headed back. They would do the last one at night before going to bed.

This book was worn out when I remembered it, they had used it so much that it was falling apart. I believe that that is what made the Salvation Army so strong in those days, being so well grounded in the word of God, the scriptures.

When they moved to the bush, we went to work at 3.30am daylight saving time, so family time was very different. However, they still managed to faithfully read the scriptures when time allowed. As we kids grew up and went to work, we developed our own Bible reading habits. I did a half-hour, sitting in the sun, after breakfast and last thing at night, I would put my Bible on a music stand and read a chapter standing up, so I wouldn't go to sleep.

Our son was riding his bike to school, when he remembered that he hadn't said his morning prayer. So, he closed his eyes to say his prayers but soon ended up back at home, being patched up from a buster. It was a reminder, as parents, that when we teach our children about spiritual things such as praying, we needed to include small facts like being able to pray with your eyes open, watch and pray is an essential spiritual and physical skill.

When my brother was doing NASHO (compulsory national service) training at Williamtown in the Air Force, it came to Christmas, and he wanted to come home to Inverell. When they were dismissed, the train that went from Newcastle to Glen Innes was long gone. So, he went out onto the highway, still in his uniform, to see whether he could thumb a ride. A fellow came along and gave him a ride on a motorbike, and he went along for a bit and had to get off there and start again.
Another chap came along and asked, "Oh, you're down at the Air Force place at Williamtown?"
He said "yeah",
"Come with me then, I'll give you a ride in an airplane".
"Where are you off to?"
He said he was going up towards Glen Innes, I forget which town but close to Glen Innes. When he got in the plane the fellow said "well, I've been up all night and I'll probably go to sleep so you've gotta keep me awake that's why I'm giving you a ride".

[2] Bus from Glen Innes to Inverell

They got up and were flying along, catching up to and then passing the train and every now and again he would doze off and my brother would have to prod him awake and keep him going. He put it down at the place where he was going, and by this time the train had got ahead of him again. He got a car ride and just as he got to Glen Innes, the train pulled out to carry on to Wallangarra. The black and white bus that goes to Inverell was also just pulling out, he hailed a taxi at the station and ran the bus down, got on the bus and he was home in time for Christmas. Not a recommended means of travelling these days.

On another occasion our second boy, Lionel, when he was finishing school at Warialda, had to go in just for the final day to pass in his books. He travelled to school on the bus, some 45kms from Bingara. So, I said to him, "you don't need to stay there all day, come home, you should be able to thumb a ride". He tried but not one person gave him a ride and he had to finish up walking the whole way from Warialda to Bingara. He was not a happy boy when he got home.

Sometimes one can have success and at other times we are not so successful, or it can be measured differently.

When my father was a young child, before he started school, he got very sick. These days we know it as appendicitis, and they just take them out. I understand the first appendix operation was carried out for one of the Kings of England about that time. They called it inflammation of the bowel in those days, and you just died a slow death. He told me that he didn't know how long he was unconscious for, but when he came to, he was so thin that his ribs were nearly sticking through his skin. He was such a long time getting better that it meant that he was a year late starting school, and they think that this was the reason for him never growing very tall. He said he could have been a jockey because of his small stature. He never ever had his appendix out, but he couldn't eat figs, fig jam, or strawberry jam which he liked as they would give him a pain where the appendix was.

In our modern day, it's wonderful, when I had my appendix out, they just put me in hospital. In those days, they gave you an anaesthetic, which made you pretty sick and it hurt and made you throw up. In my father's case, they decided that there wasn't much wrong with it, it only had a kink in it which was enough to cause the pain.

Jean's father was an old man, he'd actually retired from work, before he had to have his out. They didn't know what was wrong with him, but when they took his appendix out, they realized they had got it just in time to prevent it from bursting and causing an infection. It was some weeks before he recovered, but it just goes to show that some things can happen when you're very young or when you're very old.

[1] Kerosene Lantern

Uncle Hugh used to walk across the paddocks carrying a Lantern to see Aunty Joy, who he later married, after leaving the job he had and getting a better position. On one visit the boys, Ralph and Tom, tipped the kerosene out of his lantern and put water in it. He had to walk home in the dark.

In those days he worked at 'Wingroves' across from 'Uplands' on the Ashford Rd, Mr Wingrove had been a businessman in China and had to leave there at the time of the boxer revolt. He brought with him his family that were quite well off, and they rebuilt the home making it quite a big place. They had a Chinese cook, and a governess for their two children.

The Grays bought it after the Wingroves moved on. My uncle Ralph Gray moved over there with the family when Grandfather Gray remarried. It was built in a U shape with a servant's quarters. I remember the footpaths weren't cemented they were all fitted bricks and the servants used to walk across the back of the U shape to the

[2] Dairy herd at 'Uplands'

kitchen, pantry, and the butcher's room, it was a monstrous place. There were several large sheds for the carriages, and around the back they had one little cottage for the gardener, it was just a little room and no doubt he came round and ate with the servants. They had a big dining room, another big room in the centre with the main bedrooms off it but the servant's bedrooms were down one side.

When the Wingroves came to the area, they thought it was great fun stoking up the fires burning the scrub that had been pushed together. Lighting fires was a real adventure for them. The country was still being developed with no bulldozers, so everybody had to do it the hard way. Corn was sown behind a single farrow plough and, as my mother was a young girl, after school she had to drop the corn every step so that corn came up close together.

² Norm Morris Milking by Hand

Milking was done by hand. When they had 100 cows, you needed a lot of people to get the milking done on time. In the shed they could bale up ten cows individually at a time, so ten different milkers were working there. Milking by hand was quite something.

On one of the stony ridges there was an old shed and I remember when I was a kid, seeing the first auto-header that grandfather Gray used when they were bought out. It had a four-foot cut and was driven by a Fordson engine. This was an improvement on using eight horses. He was a great go-ahead man.

My cousin, George always wanted to ride a horse. I owned a big black horse called Tom. I took George for a ride down the paddock and on the way home I really opened the horse right up and hung on to George because we were riding bareback, and he was in a flat out gallop all the way to the house. George still talks about that ride. When he grew up, he went on to build a motel in Goondiwindi call the Gunsynd. He built sixteen motels around the country.

² Harvesting with Horses

My uncle Ralph bought a property called Warragundi, at Gragin Peak near Delungra, and it was overrun with rabbits. He killed millions of them, there were that many there that they ate everything, even the bark off the trees. It had been previously owned by a doctor with a professional manager who wore white trousers and sat on his verandah. When he went there, he put two hundred sheep on, and they all died because of the destruction caused by the rabbits. George suggested that Uncle Ralph grow wheat on shares, after the rabbits had been got rid of. George got there one evening and he had a couple of men with him, and they went right through all the flat areas and lit every log, stump and anything that would burn. When Uncle Ralph came out from town in the morning, he said he couldn't believe it, everything was alight. George was a good worker and that year they got a good crop.

George was one of those smart people; when he had a butcher shop and a fellow owed him money instead of fighting with him, he went to him and said you can't afford to feed your family, so we've got to look after your family. He said I've got some work on the sugar farm, I think you should come and work for me on Saturdays and Sundays and I'll let you gradually pay the meat off. You can still get your meat and work it off. Sure enough, the fellow and his wife were very happy, George got all his money, instead of only some of it which would have happened if he had taken action against this fellow and the family were looked after. Not many people would think like this, but George did, and he was just doing a kindness. He was a clever businessman and also full of wisdom when it comes to doing those things and thinking outside the box.

George has now become a very active Christian man making his living travelling all around the place with beehives where the honey flows are. He kept a number of Tea Boxes filled with every receipt from his motels from all the people that had stayed there over the years. One of his original ideas was to send Christian material of various sorts using the addresses off the receipts, using volunteers to help with this.

Friends

I had an old friend, Norm Downman, he lived when they were putting the railroad through to Rockhampton. There were some difficulties with the big bridge over the Comet River that took some time to get sorted. Norm's family lived 40 miles from there and his father had the mail run, which was carried out with a pack horse. He would ride one day down to Comet, delivering the mail and then he would change the horses and ride back all the way to his own block.

Norm said, "we were very well off because we had the only property that had a tin roof". The walls were made of bark. These were created by cutting bark off around the tree and then spreading it out on the ground over hot coals so it would go hard like a big sheet of fibro. He told me that, for the floor, they used ant's nests. They go and collect the Ant nest and put it down on the floor and to stop the ant's nest from going powdery, they used to get the skin of an Emu, turn it upside down so the oil would stop the dust. He said "I remember sitting there on the Emu skin mats looking at all the different patterns that the fire had made on the bark wall. We had a tank because we had a tin roof which made us very upmarket people in those days.

The amazing thing was that mum always had tea ready for my father when he came home, and I asked her years later "How did you know when dad was coming home?" She said, "we had an arrangement that, when it got near to the day that he'd be back I'd sit outside in the cool, and several kilometres down the Creek from us he used to Cooee up the Creek. He'd give several cooee's and I knew it would be another hour or so before he'd be home because he had to go over to another place and deliver their mail, they'd read the mail and then answer what needed to be answered while he waited, that way he could come home and didn't have to go back on his return trip. So, when dad got home there was a hot meal ready to put on the table for him".

Not only were there wonderful people in days gone by but in these days as well. I used to play tennis with a lady called Mrs Thompson. She was a good tennis player, a wonderfully committed Christian and originally came from New Zealand.

She had a sad life, as she had four sons and only one was still living. I asked her how this had come about, and she said, "One baby died in my arms, another was stopped up at a red light, and the load on a truck pulled up beside him, fell off and killed him, another son was so distressed he hung himself, so I only have one living son left. Through all that she still was able to express her Christian faith and love. It's one of those special things you don't often find; people who can cope with so much grief and still be a happy person.

My old friend, Peter Rivers, used to come and work at our place, his wife had dementia and on her good days he'd come over to do work for me. His wife would often ring up and say, "Where's Peter? Is Peter there?" And I'd say, "Yeah, he's here, what do you want to know, he's quite well." And as long as she knew where he was, she was happy but that was on her good days, eventually she had to go into care and Peter used to go and look after her.

He was a good builder, he'd been a builder in England and done very well over there, mixing with some of the top people. One of the prime ministers of England was a friend of his. After the war, every person that belonged to the British Empire could get somewhere to stay. They would get money to repair buildings in the form of grants. If they could repair the building up to a good living standard, they could keep the change out of whatever it was that they were given. So, Peter was quite well off, they had a little farm not far from London as well. They used to grow strawberries, and all sorts of things including pigs, which he used to sell. "I was quite well off" he said, "when I had to buy a car, I had to decide whether to buy a Mercedes or the top Volvo and safety tests said Volvos were the best", so that's what he bought.

As he got on, things changed, sad things happen to people and some of his family got into drugs and got most of his money. He was being cared for by a lady and one day he rang me and said, "Norm, I think I'm done, will you do my funeral?" I said "Oh, Peter I think I'd better come out and see you." So, Lionel, my son, took me out, it was a bit hard to find but eventually we found it up in the hills out of Cooran, where all sorts of mysterious things happen. We got there, I went in to see Peter and Lionel went to see the family he was staying with.

I said to Peter, "Now you have done a lot of kindnesses over the years, all the things that you have done have been wonderful to people, but it's not that that will get you into heaven, it's your faith in Jesus Christ. Do you believe that Jesus died for you and rose again from the dead and that's He's the saviour of the world and your saviour, if you believe that, Peter, squeeze my hand?" Well, I thought he wasn't going to let it go, he really hung on. I looked at him and I could see the veins in his neck and that his pulse was quite strong. I thought it would be a few days before he went to be with our Lord Jesus Christ, and it was. I did the service there at the house for him before his family distributed his ashes.

One of the things that amazed me was, one of the girls there was a university graduate. I asked if she would read the 23rd Psalm for me and gave it to her. She said, "That's a wonderful poem, where did you get that, I'd like to know. She had no idea, couldn't remember, or didn't know that the 23rd Psalm, "The Lord is my Shepherd, I shall not want", came out of the Bible. So, you can have well educated, academic people who do not have a real knowledge of Jesus our saviour or of the word of God.

I went to hospital once, I don't know why I was up there, but I was walking through the hospital and Doug Fraser was in there. He was a wonderful Christian fellow, he had spent time in the war at Changi prison camp and on the Burma railway line, and when he came back, he became a committed Christian during the Billy Graham Crusades. He came out of his private room and came after me, "Norm, tell me, I've spoken to one of my friends about the way of salvation and he told me what he said. "Did I get it right?" he asked. He had it right and was anxious that his friend should have a personal relationship with Jesus. I encouraged him but he was one of those fellows that really made the Christian world advance.

There was another family that we knew, when Jean and I holidayed in Burrum Heads a couple of times, because we rented their house on the sea front, which had moved closer to the house over the years, washing away the original street that was between their block and the sea at the time of purchase. The council having done some rock work to prevent further erosion.

They had been the Postmasters in Mount Isa for a long time, and it turned out that we had known one of their neighbours when we were living in Mt Isa all those years ago. Before they retired, they bought a very old house, so old that some of the six by four beams had been cut by hand with an adze. They cut it in two and moved it to a block they owned at Burrum Heads. However, the wet season was just beginning, and so they decided that they would come back the following year, get the house shifted into its proper place and do the necessary work then.

On their return, after the wet season, they discovered, to their surprise that someone, who apparently needed a house, had removed half of their future home. So, they worked with what was left, you could see where the other half of the house should have been, and made the beautiful cottage that we stayed in. She had an exhibition of preserved swordfish on the walls, which had been caught around Normanton, where they went fishing while they lived in Mt Isa. Lionel and Martin went up once or twice and helped out with some repairs because she was on her own in those days. She explained about the different kinds of swordfish, some of them with big teeth in their swords out the front and others had really fine, close teeth in their sword.

We had a friend in Bingara, he was the headmaster of the school there. His son and our third child were great friends. When he came to Bingara, he was quite young to be in charge of a school of that ranking and size. The education department had a policy of hurrying along the promotion of teachers who took appointments at schools' way out West for so many years. So, he went. He was driving to this out-of-the-way place after he'd been down to see his father, a retired butcher, who was not well. They got out as far as the crossroads at Lithgow where he needed to turn to go out West and the car stopped cold and wouldn't start again. He got out and walked over to the shop at the corner and they had the radio going. As he walked in, the radio said, "if anybody knows where this car is" and gave the registration number, which was his car, "will you please tell him to stop going West and turn around and go back to Sydney as his father has just passed away". There he was, just stepping into the shop, at the exact time the message was being broadcast, he didn't have to ask anyone for help now, he just went back to the car to tell his wife that they had to go back to Sydney. When he got in the car, it started up, and away it went and never stopped again.

This particular man, as a child, after the Christmas break when he returned to school, found out that a couple of his mates had been down to the beach for a holiday, and they had gone to the Christian beach mission. Christian Children Service Mission used to have missions on the beach in those days. His mates had got converted and when they came back, they said "You gotta get converted, become one of Jesus followers" and they talked to him about Jesus and that's how he came to know Jesus as his personal saviour and to trust in him in prayer. Years afterwards, for some reason, when we were at Bingara, he was driving on one of the back roads and there had been a bit of a storm. He said "I'm a careful driver, I've driven out West and I was coming down the hill and the sand had washed up into one of the culverts and there was a big drop there, when I put the brakes on, the car lost control and went straight towards it and was hanging over the side of the drop. I stopped and got out and went to get someone to come and get me. It was just remarkable," he said. When I got home that night, I knelt down by the side of my bed and thanked God for his protecting arm. He doesn't only protect you physically and emotionally, but spiritually as well.

One old gentleman, Vic, that I knew at Kilkivan had grown up in the outback when kids had to walk long distances to school. He told me of a scary experience he'd had as a child when the story came out about the dingo taking the baby at Uluru, or Ayers Rock, as it was known then. He told me that he knew that they would go for you because when he was a kid coming home from school, there was a bad dingo in the district and on one occasion he finished up a tree and had to wait for someone to come and get him. The dingo was just prowling around the bottom of the tree the whole time.

Vic was a wonderful fellow, he had a big family of nine children and in his latter days, after his wife died, they provided him with a house and cared for him for a number of years.

Tailors, we don't see them very much these days. You used to go in, get measured up for a suit, and they made it up in the shop. That was a full-time trade once, a lot of young fellas went into the tailoring business. One of the boys who grew up with my father was a Tailor. He was a great help to my father when he first became a fully committed Christian and then he moved away to a town on the coast called Kyogle. My dad was telling me what a help he was, they could talk to each other about spiritual matters, prayer, and scripture. I thought I should write and tell him that my father appreciated that a great deal. So, I wrote him a letter and explained to him that I was Wilfred Morris' son and Wilfred was telling me what a help he was when he was a young Christian. He never answered it, but his daughter did. Her story was just as amazing. Obviously, the letter has been discussed amongst the family. She said "I became a Christian because two young fellows were holding a Christian witness in the street at Kyogle, and I listened to them. I'm going to marry one of those boys and become a Methodist minister's wife." So, you never can tell what the effect of what you do will be.

Years afterwards, after they retired, my mum and dad went and met them in Kyogle. That's the privilege of retirement, if you can, being able to travel around and meet people.

[2] Olwyn's Wedding Party

When my youngest daughter, Olwyn, was married, one of her friends, Sue Anderson, was in the bridal party. She's an attractive, good Christian lady, of course, she's probably a grandma now. Her father was an elder in the church. He was a very interesting, committed man, and a good preacher. I knew the Anderson's were out at Millmerran, his father was well to do, and wanted to be the best at everything. When they had the dairy farm, they had the best cows, and showed them. When auto-headers came out his father decided they were a good idea. He grew wheat and all that sort of thing. His brother was a leading man in the Hereford cattle industry, touring America giving lectures and that's where he died of a brain aneurysm. I considered Neil Anderson, to be a good friend as well as an Elder. I asked him one day, "How did you become a Christian?" He said "I was feeling very depressed as a young fellow. I was shifting the header from one crop to the next and all I prayed was, God help me! I had a wonderful peace come over me when I said that. That was my first introduction to God. So, I went to the Presbyterian Church to see what I could find and learn about God. We had a very wise Presbyterian minister who said, "you, young people, start a Bible study amongst yourselves and take turns to lead the Bible study. That was a wonderful help, it taught me to read the Bible. At that time," he said, "we had a man come to the Presbyterian Church there that had come from Roma who was an alcoholic, and he was causing his wife all sorts of trouble. While at Roma his wife said to him, "look, you go down to the Salvation Army and see what they can do for you." He went down there, and they pointed him to Jesus Christ, the savour of the world who could help him overcome alcoholism. Then he had to move because of his job, and he went to the Presbyterian Church, and he was a great help to us in the Bible study. If it had not been for that Bible study, I would have spiritually withered on the vine".

It's so important not only to make a decision for Jesus but important to be able to grow in spiritual knowledge and to feed yourself because spiritual development is important. Later he did correspondence courses for preaching and he was a good preacher as well as a good elder.

I think that sometimes people make a decision but because there's nowhere for them to be fed spiritually they, using his term, wither on the vine.

Ephesians 6:18 says "with all prayer and requests, praying at all times in the Spirit, and being watchful to this end in all perseverance and requests for all the saints." It's terribly important to pray and be full of wisdom,

We have friends in Bingara who's only son became the youngest Lieutenant Colonel in the Australian military. They sent him to America to represent Australia. He married a girl from the military as well, so they both have military training, they're a good Christian couple, and are both good musicians. They looked around Brisbane, where they were stationed at the time, to find a church to attend. They found a little Presbyterian Church somewhere and decided to attend there instead of going to one of the many big churches. They said 'well, if we go to a little church, we can stimulate it", and it wasn't long after they were there, that other young couples came, and made a whole difference to the church not because they sought to have a place in a big posh church, but they wanted to be where they could have good fellowship. No wonder their mothers are very proud of them, not just because of their military expertise but also because of their Christian faithfulness.

Inverell & Surrounds

Sweeneys had a Trotter stallion, Wally Wilba, it was a very good horse and not many horses could gallop alongside him when they were doing the mile time trials at the show. He trotted faster than any of the other horses could gallop. They sent him to Brisbane for the magic mile, it was considered the top race in the country at the time, but he came second. They had another Trotter mare, Fuzzy Direct, which they used to ride, she was good, but not as good as Wally Wilba.

We had a fellow, Jim Dasey, living around Inverell that had become addicted to alcohol and when I say addicted to alcohol, I don't mean just having a beer. He was drinking metho and my dad knew him when he was a young bloke. When he was sober enough to work, he was a cook for the droving teams that shifted stock by walking them because the only transport was trains, and you can't get trains going exactly where you want them.

He came to church one night and came forward to make a decision and he was that weak that he could hardly stand on his feet. He was taken home, put in the bath, and cleaned up a bit. They got rid of the smelly clothes, and put something a bit more respectable on him, then rang the doctor and asked what to do because he was in need of medical attention. I think they put him in hospital for a while till he got better. When he got converted, he gave up his alcohol and was around for years.

My dad and mum used to go round the small churches and do weekend services. They'd take somebody to play the piano, and Jim, as he was a reasonable drummer, and he'd give his testimony. He also had a fine singing voice and used to sing, "Charge to keep I have, a God to glorify, a never dying soul to save, and fit it for the sky". My mum and dad were always great encouragers whether it was young people or old people. They did it all.

Another alcoholic that lived next to us during the war was caretaking the property because the owners were away in the services. He would get in the horrors from drinking. On one occasion, one of the milkmen was going to town early in the morning, about 5:00 o'clock to start his deliveries, and there was Aussie, walking around the telephone post with one sock on and nothing else. He also used to see pink elephants.

One night he was pretty crook and one of the neighbours was going home so they said they'd take him to his house. When they got to the house, he said, "would you mind doing me a drink? I'll show you what to do, just do it for me". So, this is the way you get educated about how some people live. He said, "there's my frying pan, put so much metho in there, so much water, get the fire going till it heats up, then put that concoction in the frying pan". They carried out his instructions, then got his mug, and he said, "now, I'll tell you when it's right, just as a little blue flame flickers across the frying pan, that's right". So, sure enough it was getting warmed up a bit and he was getting excited, "there, that's it, that's it!" They put it in the mug, he gulped it down and went out on the floor like a light. The neighbour said "I stood there, absolutely horrified. I thought I'd killed the man and there would be an inquest for sure. It was two hours before he started to come round, I was out the door and from now on, if he wants to light a fire and burn himself down that's alright".

Jackie White took fruit from his son's farm, just past our place, and would sell it in town driving backwards and forwards between there and the property and he loved to talk. He had a little black and white pony and a nice small sulky. He had false teeth, and if he'd stick them out and suck them back in when he saw you coming, you knew he was going to stop and talk. The pony got so used to it that, when you got near, the pony would stop. If you were in a hurry, you had a job to get away, he would try to keep you there forever. I remember one day, he pulled my father up and as he was talking, he said that we have ruined the country, it's no good anymore, we have to give it back to the aboriginals. The next time he saw dad, he must have thought about it a bit more, because he said that it was no point giving the country back to the aboriginals, we've ruined it. His granddaughter still lives there somewhere.

I didn't realize that there was a kind of sorghum grown very early around Inverell. When we first grew sorghum, we used to call it Milo. My father told me that his father grew sorghum and he used to cut it into sheeves, store in the shed for the cow during the winter, or when feed was a bit scarce, they used to have to thresh the seeds. His father used to put the heads in bags, gather the kids around, give them a good big strong stick, and they had to belt the bags to get the grain out. This way they got the grain out of the sheaves so they could

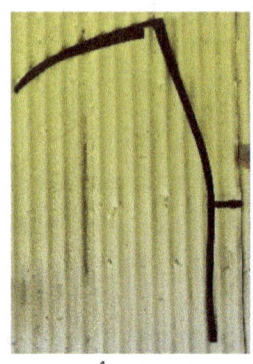

[1] Scythe

feed hay to the cows but also get the grain for sowing the next year. The kids weren't always enthusiastic about it, but it had to be done.

The crops would have been cut with the scythe. It's a blade on a big, long stick, a bit like they show in images of the grim reaper coming. We used to have one for a long time, after a while the handles get a bit loose. Dad used to cut our lucerne with it and they had to be very sharp, or they wouldn't be able to cut effectively.

[2] Sam Morris in Victoria Park, Inverell

Grandfather was a wonderful farmer or gardener really. He was the gardener in Victoria Park, and he had the first irrigation system there. He'd grow vegetables and visitors came wanting to take home some of his rhubarb. They would bring a normal traveling case to put it in, but it was so long that they just had to cut the rhubarb in half to make it fit. He grew a black grapevine on a trellis over the back verandah to help keep the place cool, a lot of grapevines were grown for that reason, but unlike today's varieties, they had a lot of seeds in them, and it was always a big job for grandma to get the seeds up to the top when she was making jam, but she would patiently scoop the seeds off with a spoon. It was great to have grapes as a kid but you're always spitting seeds out. Whatever the old skills were for growing things, Grandpa sure had them.

There was an area we called the black flat, but because so many Salvation Army people lived there, they also used to call it "Hallelujah flat", of course, some other outstanding people also lived there. One of the First World War Light horseman's family lived there and when they had an auction my dad went and purchased his Spurs. I've only got one, but his military numbers that were written on it have nearly worn off because of the use it had.

Another one of the young fellows there was always reading. Dad said no matter where he went in those days, if he was walking to town he would always be reading, and they wondered what would become of it. Eventually, he rose so far up the ranks of the Public Service to be one of the leading citizens of Australia, as it was his signature that was on the paper notes that were used as legal tender. It doesn't matter where you start from, if you apply yourself with due diligence you can finish anywhere.

I remember another incident; my dad and Charlie Harcombe were good friends. Charlie lived out on a little farm out on the Warialda Road. Occasionally, they would kill a beast between them. In those days there was no freezers in the house. If you killed a beast, you put him in the freezing rooms. They just had bags of meat hanging up, with your name on it, there was a block of wood outside and an axe, you'd go over, they'd tip your meat out of the bag, chop off a chunk of meat, put it in another bag and you'd take it home. No plastic in those days. Anyway, Dad and Charlie were killing a beast, the evening milking had to be done first and it got very late. I was at home with my mother, it got to 12:00 o'clock and nobody had arrived home, it went past 12:00 o'clock and still nobody was home, so she woke me up. She said in hindsight, "I don't know whatever I thought you were gonna do, but I sent you out looking for them". I had to ride dad's bike because dad had ridden the horse out there for the day and he had Hilt, my younger brother, with him. I had a job to ride it because I was so small. On the way there was a big old brown paper bag blowing on the side of the road and I thought it meant that they had met with a disaster, but a bit further out towards the soil conservation centre, here they were coming home, it was 2:00 o'clock in the morning. Dad and Hilt sitting on the horse and a bag of fresh meat in between them. The rest would be taken into the freezer works afterwards. Dad said that he saw the light, (the push bikes had what they called domino that ran on the tire creating the electricity for the light, the faster you went the better the light was) but because I wasn't travelling very fast the light was not very bright and he said to Hilt, "I think that's my bike coming". I'd ride a horse over to the freezing works, once a week to collect our meat. The cordial factory, ice cream factory, and freezing works were all there near the Tingha bridge run by Ben Wade.

When the depression eased off a bit, dad used to take a horse for someone that couldn't manage it and we'd get them going for them. I remember this one particular horse, Bob, I think we called him. We had him for a good while because he took a lot to get organized. He'd grown up as a foal around town and he was the biggest rouge, not vicious, but he knew all the tricks. Dad had him over in a twenty-five acre paddock we had where Froud Street is now. The condition was that we could have it free of charge as long as we kept the fences up to keep cattle in and cut the Bathurst burrs. Connected to it we had two or three acres which belonged to the Burge brothers, one owned Palo Alto, the other owned a block of land that had a vacant house and a couple of sheds including a milking shed and a small yard for the calves, which we also looked after. We had this horse there and, if he thought there was better grass over a fence, he'd rare up and jump over it. Dad looked out one evening and thought 'he's over that fence' but then thought he couldn't be, he was seeing things. However, he was, and stayed there all night till dad went out in the morning. Dad told me that he'd eaten every bit of grass he could reach right down to the dirt. The horse was intelligent enough to never do it again. We had to get him going, and I had to ride him every afternoon after school along the roads and laneways. He wouldn't buck but he'd stand on his hind legs to make you slip off. Dad told me to hit him between the ears when he did this, with a stock whip, but I was struggling to hang on, let alone give him a hit. Once we got him sorted, we then had to train him to pull a sulky, which we did, and he ran in one of the milk carts for years until motor vehicles came in. Dad loved horses, he had good animal sense and knew how to make things happen.

When we went dairy farming, we got our cows from all sorts of places. We called them the "league of nations". Dad was very fond of the Guernsey herd; he had some good Guernsey bulls. Dad had a very strict rule with his cows, on its first calf, if everything was normal, it had to give a 15 pound (one and half gallons) of milk a day. He just had a set of ordinary house scales at the dairy and any cow that came in, that was the test she had to pass. He considered that, if she didn't pass for some reason, she might be sick or have had a bad calving. The milk was weighed, and for that reason he sold a lot of cows, people would say, "why are you selling that good looking cow?" He said, "it's not the looks I want, it's the milk. I like good looks too but it's the milk that I want first". So, before he sold his dairy, he had the best production per cow of any herd selling to the milk factory; he had 30 cows producing 90 gallons of milk a day and some of the others had 100 that wouldn't have been producing any more than 120 gallons. When he was selling the dairy, one buyer came out to look at the herd and dad had a nice bunch of heifers. Mr Sweeney, who was a great cattle Judge, when asked about all the young stock, said, "this man has done all the hard work, if you buy them you will have a good lot of cattle for years to come". They didn't usually milk cows before the sale, so it made them look as if they had a big lot of milk, but dad milked his cows before the sale, and they still had a lot of milk. They bought him a good price. He was a very successful Stockman, my father, he might have been a bootmaker by trade, but he had natural animal sense.

Before we went farming, Dad had a house cow running on that 25 acres and he had a block of wood that he used to sit on to milk her in the corner of the

paddock. He'd go over there to milk her. I think there was a Policeman in town who thought he had the best cow around, and he came into dad's boot shop and said, "they tell me you've got a good house cow, Wilfred".
Dad said, "Oh, she's alright".
"How much milk does she give?"
"Well," he said, "I go over there with a four-gallon kerosene tin and when I'm finished, I've got a job to carry it home without slopping it over the edge".
"Oh, my cow's flat out to be that good".
One of the cows had a bull calf by a bull from Hawkesbury agriculture college, owned by a relative. He was the guernsey bull that dad bred his herd off.

After the depression, we got a pony and sulky. My Grandfather Piggott was a great preacher. He was on the Bundarra Shire council, but he was also preacher for the Methodist church and used to go around preaching. One of the places he used to go preaching was Copeton, where the Copeton Dam is now. Dad told me to go and pick-up grandma Morris, over in William Street, and drive her out to Copeton which had been deserted. I have no idea of how I knew how to get there now, I suppose grandma knew, but anyway, we drove out there, but the church was all that was left. We got into the church, and it was completely empty except for the old pedal organ, and I remember grandma going up onto the platform and looking at the old organ. I don't remember us taking lunch, but we would have done that as a matter of course, and then I drove back. We did all sorts of funny things as kids.

They had been getting black diamonds from there and they never really learnt to cut them until the space program got going. They had to have hard stuff for when they were coming back into the atmosphere. A lot of the things we use on emery and cutting wheels now are the by-product of the space program.

Years ago, before we had modern machinery, like we have today, the farmers used to sow their wheat by hand. My grandfather Gray used to be pretty good

[2] Grandfather Thomas Gray

at it, he'd ride a horse with a butt of wheat and broadcast it out to the right and the left. He was so good at it that you couldn't tell where one side joined the other, he'd go over it afterwards with the harrows and the paddocks produced good crops of wheat. My mother was told, years later by others, about how good he was.

I've even done it myself that way, with Rye grass in small paddocks as the ground was too uneven and we wanted to get the seed right up to the fences, it was easier to walk the paddock instead of using the tractor, and we managed to get pretty good at it as well. This was the way seeds were sown in Jesus' time and sometimes the old way can be practical, even in today's world.

During the war, some of our older cousins went to fight. One in particular spent a lot of time as a soldier. Soldiers didn't get paid much, a shilling a day, or something like that. When they came home, they got what they called their deferred pay. His family was living out on a property and didn't have anything. His mother and father were down in Sydney, while his father was having an operation. The kids left behind were hungry, as they could only get eggs or kill a chook to eat, but that was about all they had. They came to my father and said, "how do we write to mum and not worry her but tell her that we're short of food?" My father was a great diplomat and composed a letter for them which said that they were home and things weren't too bad. That seemed to satisfy them. Then, just at that point, their oldest brother, who had been away in the war, came home and was horrified at how close they were to starving. He went back to town, I'm not sure what vehicle they used, I know that at one stage they had an old Dodge ute, but anyway they went back to town. He had a big spend up with his deferred pay, so they got food at the last minute. Mum and dad didn't know, until they come back, how bad things were but that sort of thing often happened in those days and was part of the struggle, for many, during the war.

When the war was on, they made planes in Australia, they didn't look somewhere else for them. One of the things that I remember was we had to put out all our aluminium saucepans and things that we had out on the road, and they'd come along in a military vehicle and collect them all up to make aeroplanes for the war effort. It was strange to think that your aluminium things were out there flying around the world somewhere helping to keep our country safe from invasion.

In the book of Joel, it has this: "What the swarming locust has left, the great locust has eaten. What the great locust has left, the grasshopper has eaten. What the grasshopper has left, the caterpillar has eaten." (Joel 1:4)

Grasshoppers: I remember as a kid the grasshoppers swarming along the ground. They'd hatch out and all these locusts, before they flew, would crawl along the ground eating everything as they went, leaving the ground bare. We used to have to go out with bags soaked in sump oil on a big stick and a pitchfork or something. As they moved along in the swam, we had to go along with a burning bag and burn as many as we could. Now they fly over with insect spray. I remember one year, when I was at school, the flying grasshoppers were so bad that the sky was black all day, we didn't see the sun, they were just that thick. They would even eat green curtains irrespective of the kind of the material they were made of. Modern technology has done away with a lot of those things but the grasshoppers, as we call them here in Australia, can still eat a lot of crops if they are not stopped.

My father was a bootmaker in the town of Inverell, that had about 10,000 people in those days. My father would buy all sorts of different leathers; soft leathers and kangaroo hide for special dancing shoes or pumps. Stylish ladies

² Wilfred Morris in his Boot shop

would wear them. To make these, my father used to have to turn them inside out and sew them up by hand so that, when they were turned back the right way, there was no sign that that they joined the upper part to the sole of the shoe. It looked as if it was all put together in one. I understand that they are now only used for dancing.

The travellers used to come around selling all the different leathers, the big leather, which was the full hide of the beast, I remember as a kid, dad had a backroom behind his shop and if I was tired, he'd put one of these hides down, flat on the floor and I used to sleep there. You could occasionally see the holes left by ticks and the mark on them from where the beast had been branded.

He asked the leather traveller one day, in a little town of ten thousand people, how many people used leather. The man said there were 23 shops he had to call on. There was very little rubber available, so leather was even used for mining.

When I was a boy, there was a number of slaughter yards around Inverell, my hometown, where the butcher killed his meat, every little town had at least one. The butcher would go out early in the morning and he'd kill one or two bullocks, cows, sheep and pigs and dress them ready for the customers to come in. They must have been wonderfully skilled fellows. There was a slaughterhouse cart, which came into Inverell to 'Girls Butcher Shop' (it was where the National Bank is now). The cart was backed in underneath the shop and they'd winch all the bodies up. If you were there at 6:00 o'clock you could get a lamb's fry for sixpence. My mother sometimes sent me down with sixpence to get a lamb's fry for breakfast. I'd take it home and she'd cut it up and we'd have lamb's fry, now I'm a bit indulgent and I don't mind lamb's fry with bacon, but I don't remember having any bacon with it back then.

I saw something exceptional happen down there behind that shop that I have never forgotten. They had a house below there, where the yardman lived. It was his job to look after the horses, carts, and the yard, because in those days, you could give an order to the butcher and the meat would be delivered to your home, and left somewhere just like the milkman, baker, and grocer did. The man who looked after this yard was Mr Truman, he was a reliable worker but, on the weekends, he'd get into the grog and get drunk. This particular Sunday evening, we were standing at the hotel opposite, on the corner, where Otho and Byron streets join, and out comes Mr Truman. He must have been drunk and playing up a bit inside and he staggered out into the driveway. He wasn't very good on his feet, but he was standing up you'd have to say that. His wife came out after him, she was a big substantial woman, she leaned over, pulled a paling off the fence, and gave him a couple of good broad cuts across the behind with it. It echoed up Otho Street just like a gun. They had a number of children and later, some of them ran the caravan park at Texas.

In those days there was no such thing as stainless-steel cutlery. So, each Saturday morning, it was my father's job to shine all the knives, forks, and spoons on a sandsoap block. He had to rub and shine them. They had wooden handles and the forks got very sharp, with the constant cleaning. It wasn't a job that he enjoyed very much, but it had to be done and taught him stickability and perseverance.

The other thing that my father had was a pocket watch, but he never had a wristwatch. As we got older, my brother and I took a couple of trips to Sydney. On one journey we took part in Children's Special Mission events at Thirroul Bay and then went to Sydney to visit some relatives. I decided to buy my father a wristwatch. It had to be wound up each day and cost me the equivalent of two weeks wages. It was made to last, as it was still working when he died, in 1977, and was returned to me, however, the back of it was almost paper thin from being on his wrist.

In the old days there were many homemade breweries. There was one particular brewery on the way out to Gilgai, after you go up Strahley's ridge, on the left-hand side. It was reputed to be wonderful stuff, even alleging that if a willy wagtail got a drink, it would look for a turkey gobbler to fight. Such was its reputation for making someone to feel like something they weren't. They also had a piggery attached and they would feed the left-over barley to them, if some of the beer went off or sour, they would feed that to the pigs to get rid of it. The sows would have a big feed and just go and lay down to get over their hang-over, but the little suckers would drink it and start walking around on their hind-legs. Such are the effects of alcohol on both animals, birds, and humans. Maybe this is where the term pickled pork came from.

[1] Post and Rail Fence

My mother was a great visitor to people who were lonely. One particular person was Mr. Barnes and his daughter Pearl. They lived behind the shop near the Ross Hill School. I remember Mr. Barnes taking me down to his shed and showing me his old tools that he used as a post and rail fencer, which he made a living at for many years. I was too young, at the time, to realize what the tools were and how they were used but as I got older, I managed to work out some of what he had. I didn't know what an expert he was until years afterwards when we had neighbours who had a Guernsey stud. Two of their bull yards had been built by Mr Barnes many years before. Mr Freighter used to say he was a remarkable man. He's gone, but his workmanship still stands as a witness to his skills, and he never wasted time, he would even clock off just to go down into the bush, where you had to go if you needed to go the toilet. When asked about it, he declared that it was his private time, and he would not charge for it. His work was done for his clients but also for God, making him not only clever but also very honest.

In Inverell there was a shallow crossing, called Gillespie's Crossing, across the river near where the low walking bridge was that allowed people to get across to the black flat, or south side, where a large amount of gravel used to be collected and was used in cement or gravel footpaths. If you had a horse and sulky with steel tires, instead of rubber ones, in hot dry weather, the tires would get loose as the wood dried out and shrunk. So, they would drive the sulky into the crossing and allow the wood to soak so it would expand tightening up the tires again.

The mailman, in our day if you lived out of town, used to not only bring your letters, but also your bread, newspapers, and orders. There was one mailman, who was very prompt, his run went from Ashford, along the Ashford Road, past Windgrove. He was so precise that they said you could set your watch by him, because he would only be one minute either side of the usual time, giving him the nickname of Dead-on-time-Bailey.

We met up with him again when we lived to Bingara, where he had a mail run. I took his wife to Inverell one day, as she wanted a lift and when we went through Little Plain, she told me about how her father had a general store there, while she was growing up, selling billies, food, kerosene, and lanterns. The village was quite a substantial place then.

The school and memorial hall was at the one end, with the general store halfway along the road, the Post office/exchange was at the other end of the town. The telephones in those day were called 'party lines' which were a great part of life back then. The one line would go out from the exchange and service several properties at the same time. So, when a call came in for someone on the line, the exchange would ring it once for one property, twice for someone else, or a long and short ring for another. Sometimes, either by accident or design, if you picked up the phone you could listen in to other people's conversations. On one particular line, they knew who had the reputation of listening into other people's calls, so at the end of a particular conversation, the caller finished the call by saying, "Goodbye, Goodnight Doris" and Doris replied, "Goodnight", having been caught out listening in when she shouldn't have.

The memorial halls, many having been built after the WWI, consisted of a galvanized shed, with kitchen and fireplace. One cloudy miserable day, as I was driving between Delungra and Inverell, I saw a swagman walking along the road. I offered him a lift, and he accepted, asking me to drop him off at the hall at Little Plain, he knew how to get in and take shelter as he seemed to think that it would rain for a couple of days, which proved to be right at the time. He told me about his three-year circuit that he did. He was the last swagman I remember seeing, and the hall is also no longer there.

[2] Swaggie

Swaggies were common, particularly during the depression. One story I heard was that it was pretty dry, and this particular swaggie had a horse, making him rather well off as swaggies go. He wanted to spell his horse in a farmer's paddock. So, he made himself a stick-horse and rode it up to the farmer. I'm told the conversation went along the lines of:
"Would you mind if I let my horse use your front paddock down by the road for the night?"
"No, that would be alright," the farmer thinking 'this guy's a bit simple' or these days we'd say challenged. The swaggie turned around and rode the stick-horse back down the driveway and while he was putting his real horse in the paddock, the farmer came along and discovered that there was a real animal on his feed, he said: "Hey, what are you doing?" "I'm spelling my horse in your paddock, you just said I could". The farmer, being a good sport, let it go.

In the coastal areas, because of the moisture, when something dies, it disintegrates quickly and that's something we had to learn when we came to Gympie from the inland. One of the old country songs tells of putting retired horses out in the long paddock. The long paddock is a reference to the reserves around the country. Moree was a different story, being dry and hot, and once, in that region, a horse had been retired to the long paddock where he died. He lay there on the ground, disintegrated except for his skin which stayed on his bones and some fellow with a great sense of humour came along, propped him up against a tree then put a nosebag on him as if he was having a feed.

One night, a mum wanted to go out and husband said, "It's alright, I'll stop home look after the kids tonight, you go out and do whatever you want". He told her that he'd put the kids to bed, thinking he'd have a quiet night by putting them to bed early and watch his favourite program downstairs, everything would be sweet. He went up with the children, put them to bed and heard their prayers, which is what mother normally does. It didn't take very long, then he came down, got into his comfy chair and was just in the process of starting to watch his favourite program when one of the boys sung out and said "Dad, I want a drink of water". "Alright" he said, so, dad got a glass of water, took it up and gave him a drink. He hadn't long got back in his comfy chair, when the boy called out again, "Dad, I want a drink of water". So, he gave him another drink, and this happened two or three times. He'd want a drink of water then he'd want to go to the toilet, having dad home was something special. At last, his father put him into bed and said, "don't sing out again, or I'll come up and give you a spanking". After he'd settled back in his chair, the boy sang out and said, "Dad, when you come up to give me a spanking, will you bring a glass of water." So, it's one thing to be prayerful and offer guidance, but you've got to do it with wisdom, perseverance, and supplication. It's part of being the Saints of God.

In the early days, they had to harvest the corn by hand, they had to pick the cobs and put them in the shed and then, after work, they went back to the

[2] Harvesting at 'Uplands'

shed to thresh the cobs, until they got a machine that would do it for them. These days the headers do it all, doing away with a lot of jobs but making it more sensible and easier.

Parks

When we lived in Parks, there was a businessman who ran a departmental store. His name was Jack Burke. He was a very able man. He didn't have to run his business really, as he didn't need the money, but he ran it for great fun. His office was set up so he could see all over his store, every Department could be seen from his office. He'd sit there and say, "There's Mrs So-and-So, give her a pair of stockings." Then he'd look around and say, "There's Mr So-and-So, make sure he gets the right sort of shoes and he'd be talking to his staff and customers while he was up there with the loudspeaker system in every department. His opposition would get upset and ring him saying, "You can't do this Jack, you run your specials and you say you won't be undersold. There's nothing there that they can buy cheaper anywhere else in Parks," and he'd say, "Well, I'm doing it, and I've been doing it for a long time". The great beneficiaries, of course, were the citizens. They got cheap things and that was his policy. Burkes will not be undersold.

As a side note, the parking at his store was out in the open and he used to come to work in his latest model car but, every now and again, if the weather was good, he'd drive his restored Rolls Royce sports car. He was a wonderful person for the community as well as good for the customers.

[2] The Chapmans

The Chapmans got married in Parks. Mrs Chapman was an Edwards and her family had made their money in England. They used to specialise in tea, delivering it in gold packets to the people in and around London. They used to have a horse and cart with special harnesses, so they looked really flash. After they sold out and came to Australia, I asked her where they got the tea from. She told me that it came in big, three-foot by three-foot wooden tea boxes, some of these busted on the wharf, and they used to sweep up the leaves, put it into their special packets, and people thought they were getting a specialty tea.

Not everything is what it seems.

[1] A Set of Scales

When we were at Parks, I used to have to go to Peak Hill once a month. On the way out there, was a family that I knew pretty well. They owned a number of properties around Alectown. It had been an old gold mining place. There was a shop where they used to buy gold and you could see a hole worn in the counter where they put the gold before they weighed it.

This farmer and his two sons were fencing when I called in to see them on one trip. The three of them were standing posts, for a three barbed wire fence. In those days we used a bit and auger which you turned by hand to bore the holes in the posts for the wire, which meant that the bit was a large one. I said: "I can do that while you stand the post". The three of them were standing the post pretty fast and by the end of it I was boring the hole in the narrowest part of the post.

After that they offered me lunch to get over the work as it had been a long time since I'd done any fencing.

I remember a lady there, who was wise. She said that "you can't have everything going smoothly all the time, you have to have a bit of activity or opposition because it's not good for you". She would tell an old story from America about exporting fish to Europe. They packed the live fish in saltwater containers and shipped them, but when they arrived, they were no good, they were sloppy and too fat. At last, someone hit on the idea that, while they were in their native environment, a catfish was what caused them trouble. So, they put a couple of catfish in the containers which chased the fish around during their trip to Europe and when they arrived, they were fine and lovely to eat.

If you are having troubles, it's like having a catfish in your tank. It keeps you fit, spiritually, physically, and emotionally. If the going is easy you will just get fat and sloppy.

One of the people there had a girl staying with them for a while, they also had a son and a daughter. The country around Peak Hill is very flat. So, when floods come through, the water just walks across the country, soaking into the ground which is wonderful for the soil. It doesn't run off in a rush like it does in Gympie where the country is steeper. When one of their dams went dry, they got a yellow belly out of it which was too fat because he hadn't been very active.

They also had a very good dam that hadn't been dry for many years, which had crayfish in it. This girl was sitting there catching them, she had a Kerosene tin and little pieces of meat on lengths of string. She tied them to her toes and finger, and as the crayfish nibbled on the meat, she was able to pick them up and put them in the Kerosene tin. That evening we had crayfish, just like lobster, for dinner.

[2] Norm Morris Delivering 'The War Cry'

I had a businessman I used to visit at Peak Hill. I used to give him the Salvation Army newspaper, The War Cry. One day he pointed to a photo in the paper and asked: "Do you know this fellow?"

I said "Noo... Oh yes. I do, I met him years ago in Mt Isa."

"Oh", he said "I knew him back in the days during the war. He was a Jew. He managed to convince the German's that he wasn't a Jew because that would send him to the incinerator. He had them convinced that he was a New Zealander. He even had a photo of a New Zealand family he used to carry with him and that he was there in Germany as a New Zealander. The last time I saw him, after the war was over and peace had been declared, he was wheeling a pram with his belongings in it near the road along the railway line. I often wondered where he went and here he is in the Salvation Army paper. You know him?"

Yes, I had met him in Mt Isa some years ago, he was still trotting about doing his thing and very resourceful and capable at looking after himself. He needed to be after going through all that.

You just never know who you will meet, or where they have come from or what they might have been through to get there.

When we went to Parks, I had the latest technical thing at the time, in recording, it was called a TechniCorder and was a big suitcase or port. The lady who told me about the fish had two daughters, one was getting married to a young man, whose surname was Redman. When I spoke to him, I discovered that we knew his grandmother, in Canowindra.

[1] Recording Machine

The lady asked me to record the wedding, which meant that I had to hide down behind the pulpit with this great solid machine. We had to put out a microphone, which in those days had to be put on a cushion, so it wouldn't pick up the vibrations and produce static. This was my first recording experience. If the tape still exists, there would be nothing around that it could be played on.

The last I heard of the Redman family, they were running the grocery store at Peak Hill, which probably doesn't exist anymore either.

The Mayor of Parks was a man named Cecil Moon, he and his wife would often drink quite a bit, particularly at weekends. She would get her hair done every morning, and Cecil would carry out his mayoral duties. One day, Cecil said to me, "Parks in the only place that has three full moons on the weekend. I'm full, my wife is full, and there's a full moon in the sky."

Parks had the satellite dish, which was reasonably new when we were there, that was part of the first moon landing, and I knew one of the staff that worked there. He was a quiet sort of bloke who didn't say too much about what he could do. When he heard that we were having the Parramatta Salvation Army Band visiting, he suggested that, if the times worked out, he would take them out to have a look around the dish as it was good for Parks to let people know about it. Which he did.

One little known fact about the moon landing is that, before the men left Apollo 11, they had communion. It seems to be that people who do outstanding things often give their first loyalty and love to Jesus Christ, our Saviour. He said, "as often as you do this, do this in remembrance of Me". I guess that they must have wondered if they would ever come back to earth, as it was such a new venture. They did, of course, and the rest is history.

Sue's Story
As told by Sue Williams

Henry and Lexy Homan were a young married couple while World War II was on and everyone needed to do their part.

Henry was in the military forces and Lexy was working in an ammunition factory. The stress caused Lexy to miscarry and become ill. As part of her recovery program, she was sent to the beach to convalesce.

[2] Lexy Homan

One afternoon, she went and laid on the beach, when a German plane swooped in strafing the beach, guns blazing, very low and close. This seemed like the end for Lexy. Suddenly the guns stopped, the plane banked and disappeared into the English sky. Lexy hurried (as much as her frailty would let her) for shelter. Telling her carers how close the bullets came. Her looks would have said more than her words conveyed. When Lexy's health improved, she went back to the ammunition factory to make bullets to use against the Germans (there are no winners in war).

When the Homan's first child was born, bombs were falling on London. One came very close as Lexy was on her way to the maternity hospital. The shock wave actually lifted the vehicle.

When the war was over in Europe and the pacific, Henry did some service with the occupational forces in Japan. Later, he and Lexy both got work in England where a brother and sister were added to the family. They came to Australia as assisted migrants in 1958.

Sue, the eldest daughter married in 1964. They built a new home in Melbourne and had a family of boys.

Not all was good and there was a divorce. (One of Sue's blessings is that all four boys have marriages that have lasted).

She had to find a place to live. She saw an ad for a home in Kilkivan and could not believe how cheap it was. Her father brought her up to Kilkivan to inspect it and she bought a house and two acres for $4500. One reason for cheap properties was there were few or no permanent jobs in the village. Later her father and mother built a home there as well. Her father grew vegetables on one of the acres and sold them locally.

She had to do multiple jobs, cook at the pub, cleaning, child minding, washing, and ironing. There were often hard times when she needed God's help. Her mind went back to the decision she made to follow Jesus in the hostel where they first stayed on coming to Australia.

The Berean Bible college students came to the hostel regularly and held services. She was to prove God's guidance and love in later years.

She believed Christian teaching was important, so she fitted into her program the teaching of Religious Education (RE) at the school. She was a good and effective teacher. Years later, one of her students drove all the way to Kilkivan to thank her, "I've got it!" they told her. "What you taught us in RE. I'm an all-in Christian now".

On another occasion, a travelling evangelist was coming to town, so Sue put on a home group meeting for him, inviting all the church people. She even had new carpet put down in the lounge and living area. Her youngest son met a man near the pub, very drunk. "Come up to mum's, there's a party on. She's known for her suppers." The drunk managed to make it up the stairs into the home. Sue spent the entire meeting thinking that he'd be sick all over the new carpet. Instead, he made the best decision of his life and asked Jesus Christ into his life. He left town, and later let them know he'd been baptized and became a member of the Baptist church in the major city.

Sue's caring and helping the needy in Kilkivan made her aware of their different needs. Her secretarial experience came to the fore and she wrote down a list. Something like:

1. Some need nourishing meals.
2. Some need carers.
3. Other cleaners to come in.
4. Means to get to medical appointments.
5. Nurses to do professional care.
6. Social get-togethers with people of their age.

Sue never imagined she would be able to do these things. Years later the federal government launched a project to keep people in their homes longer called "Community aged care program". Kilkivan was selected as the district trial project and Beaudesert as the nursing home trial. A councillor on the Kilkivan Shire Council at the time stated, "We have a lady doing that sort of thing at her own expense. She's the one to put in charge." Sue was put in charge of making the Community Age Care Program work. She now went back to the list she had made years before. The project developed from there. She was paid to do it with a car supplied.

The project was such a success that the principles were adopted and are now available to those assessed as being in need all over Australia. We have many groups doing this work in every state patterned on the lessons learnt by this Christian lady that came to Australia at fourteen years old. The daughter of the lady a German pilot let live on an English beach and who narrowly missed being bombed on the way to the maternity hospital.

In their later years, Lexy and Henry loved to travel. The young lady that was given life on the beach now made the most of living. They still had a home in Kilkivan and, as their daughter and family lived there, they would often return to see friends and loved ones. Lexy was visiting her friend, Molly, who was a prolific reader of real-life stores. She had been reading a German pilot's memories and experiences of World War II. One of the memories was of a girl he let live on the beach in England. He wrote, "there she was lying on the beach. I made my strafing run. I had her in my sights. Cannons going, when flashing into my mind came the thought, she's about my wife's age and I have two children. She could be my loved one. I stopped the guns and banked up and away into the English sky and back to base." Lexy's expression changed in amazement. "That girl was me", she lived again the heart stopping moments, even though she was on the other side of the world in a little village in Queensland, Australia. The refrain of the hymn by Lida S Leech became real.

Someday He'll make it plain to me
Someday when I his face will see
Someday from tears I shall be free
For someday I shall understand.

Inspired from 1 Corinthians 13:12. For now we see in a mirror darkly, but then face to face. Now I know in part, but then I shall know just as I also am known.

Other Books by Helen Brown

All these books, with the exception of Whispers from on High, are available as eBooks.

Turning Water into Wine
100 Stories of God's Hand in Life

More Water into Wine
100 Stories of God's Hand in Life

Still More Water into Wine
100 Stories of God's Hand in Life

Reflections
Australian Stories from my Father's Past

365 Glasses of Wine
Short Devotionals for each day of the year

Conversations with Myself – Volume 1
100 Stories of Hope, Faith and Determination

Whispers from on High
Poems and short stories

Christmas Journeys
Helen's debut novel

Follow Helen Brown on:
Facebook: https://www.facebook.com/HelenBrownCollection/

Instagram: https://www.instagram.com/helen_brown_books/

Pinterest: https://www.pinterest.com.au/helenbrown58726/

Connect with Reading Stones for other great reads:
https://www.facebook.com/Reading-Stones-Publishing-and-Editing-Services-252366958298920

www.ingramcontent.com/pod-product-compliance
Lightning Source LLC
Chambersburg PA
CBHW071408290426
44108CB00014B/1741